Chloe's
Vegan Italian
Kitchen

Chloe's Vegan Italian Kitchen

150 Pizzas, Pastas, Pestos, Risottos,
& Lots of Creamy Italian Classics

CHLOE COSCARELLI

ATRIA PAPERBACK

New York   London   Toronto   Sydney   New Delhi

ATRIA PAPERBACK

A Division of Simon & Schuster, Inc.
1230 Avenue of the Americas
New York, NY 10020

All photography by Teri Lyn Fisher except:
Cover photography by Miki Duisterhof.
Additional photography by Miki Duisterhof (pages x, 87, 150, 236, and 240)
Chloe, Shelley, and Don Coscarelli (pages ii, v, xiv, xvi, 5, 6, 22, 28, 30, 35, 43, 51, 63, 65, 74, 78, 81, 85, 91, 99, 105, 107, 123, 149, 154, 157, 176, 181, 187, 206, 210, 212, 214, 248, 262, and 272)
Robert Raphael (page 173)

First Atria Paperback edition September 2014

ATRIA PAPERBACK and colophon are trademarks of Simon & Schuster, Inc.

For information about special discounts for bulk purchases, please contact Simon & Schuster Special Sales at 1-866-506-1949 or business@simonandschuster.com.

The Simon & Schuster Speakers Bureau can bring authors to your live event. For more information or to book an event contact the Simon & Schuster Speakers Bureau at 1-866-248-3049 or visit our website at www.simonspeakers.com.

Interior design by Kris Tobiassen / Matchbook Digital

Manufactured in China

10 9 8 7 6 5 4 3 2 1

Library of Congress Cataloging-in-Publication Data

Coscarelli, Chloe.
   Chloe's Vegan Italian Kitchen : 150 pizzas, pastas, pestos, risottos, and lots of creamy Italian classics / Chloe Coscarelli.
      pages cm
   Includes index.
1. Cooking, Italian. 2. Vegan cooking.   I. Title.   II. Title: Italian kitchen.
   TX723.C68174 2014
   641.5945--dc23
                                                      2013045234
ISBN-13: 978-1-4767-3607-5
ISBN: 978-1-4767-3608-2 (ebook)

TO MY DAD,

There's an Italian expression:
"Papa' e re a desinaren non si fan mai aspettare."
It means: Never make a dad wait too long for his food.

I can't say I've never made you wait, but
hopefully I've made it up to you with
seconds and thirds.

Ti voglio bene!

CONTENTS

APPETIZERS
(ANTIPASTI)

VEGETABLES
(VERDURE)

★ *Chloe's Favorite Recipe*
(GF) = *Can be made Gluten-Free*

Soups and Salads
(Zuppa e Insalata)

Pizza, Focaccia, and Panini
(Pizza, Focàccia, e Panini)

Viva la Pasta

The Main Course
(Secondo Piatti)

Desserts
(Dolci)

MAKE-YOUR-OWN BASICS
DOUGH, SAUCES, AND VEGAN CHEESE

INTRODUCTION
IF YOU CAN'T GO TO ITALY, LET ITALY COME TO YOU

Ciao friends!

We may have met before in my other cookbooks, *Chloe's Kitchen* or *Chloe's Vegan Desserts*, and so we meet again! When it comes to Italian food, it's amore. I love anything that's hot and doughy, creamy and cheesy, or topped with fresh heirloom tomatoes and basil. In my heaven, you drink pesto sauce with a straw and include noodles on the breakfast table.

And while I love dining out at Italian restaurants, whether fancy and romantic or casual family style, there is something about home-cooked Italian food that cannot be replaced. Ordering vegan at Italian restaurants often means pasta marinara or pizza without the cheese. But in *Chloe's Vegan Italian Kitchen*, you can find recipes for creamy Pasta Carbonara with Shiitake Bacon (page 133) or Crumbled Sausage and Mozzarella Pizza (page 92). That's right, these recipes are *all vegan*!

So let me back it up a little. Eating vegan means avoiding meat, fish, dairy, and eggs. This means no artery-clogging animal fats or greasy, cheesy dishes that put you into a food coma. My vegan recipes use unprocessed, healthy, plant-based ingredients that are good for your body and kinder to our sweet animal friends. In other words, you can feel great while you stuff your face!

"WHAT? Are you *crazy*? Is meatless, cheeseless Italian food even possible?"

You bet! I come from a hungry Italian family, and we take our pasta very seriously. I've taken family recipes from generations back and "veganized" them into their most delicious meat- and dairy-free form. I also put my own Italian twist on some American classics like onion rings, quesadillas, and more!

My family is originally from the Calabria region of southern Italy. However, our roots are Sicilian, as the most distant ancestor we can trace is Caterina Palermo, who was born in 1683 in Sicily.

My great-grandfather Angelo Coscarelli emigrated from Lago to escape being drafted into the Italian Army during World War I. Though born Angelo Coscarella, upon arriving at Ellis Island and then ultimately settling in Pittsburgh, Pennsylvania, he changed his name to Coscarelli. Ironically, immediately upon arrival in the States, Angelo was drafted into the U.S. Army and served honorably as a doughboy in WWI.

My great-grandmother Antoinette Petrone Coscarelli was the original chef of our family. Her great holiday meals are legendary. From her small kitchen in her home on Mount Washington, she literally worked around the clock to prepare the feasts for our large extended family. The meals would last all day. We would sit at the grand dining room table for breakfast and before we got up, Aunt Gilda was bringing out the lunch dishes. We spent hours at that table!

The dishes she was known for include fried zucchini; a terrific fresh tomato salad with onions, garlic, and parsley; and amazing fresh pastas. Many of her recipes have been "veganized" for this book. Antoinette had her own home vegetable garden in the yard and her favorite was fresh Swiss chard.

With that bit of history out of the way, here are my three promises to you:

1. **Every recipe is super easy.** If you have any questions along the way, just contact me on Twitter or Facebook for help. I am with you in your kitchen!

2. **Your friends and family won't believe your cooking is vegan.** I've tested these recipes at some two hundred dinner parties, and the response is always, "Are you sure there's no cheese in this?"

3. **Vegan Italian food is a love potion.** I've cooked my way into so many people's hearts with these recipes. There is no gesture more sincere than a home-cooked Italian dinner for a parent, child, neighbor, or potential love interest (it works like a charm!). My recipes were made for you with love, so cook them with love, and watch people devour them with smiles on their saucy faces.

Whether you're a pro chef or have never boiled water before, *bravissimo* for picking up this book and following your foodie dreams. So relax, grab yourself a sous chef—whether it be your dog or a glass of vino—and turn your kitchen into Trattoria da (insert your name)!

Con amore,
Chloe

PASTAGRAM

1
5
9
2
6
3
7
4

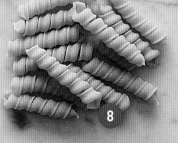

8

1. cavatappi
2. capunti
3. orecchiette
4. rigatoni
5. farfalle
6. fusilli
7. gemelli
8. cannolicchi
9. bucatini

CHLOE'S ITALIAN LESSON

hello, good-bye—*ciao*

formal good-bye—*arrivederci*

please—*per favore*

thank you—*grazie*

nice to meet you—*piacere*

good morning—*buongiorno*

good evening (be sure to say that to anyone passing by)—*buona sera*

good night—*buona notte*

I am vegetarian—*sono vegetariano/a*

I am vegan—*sono vegano/a*

without cheese—*senza formaggio*

without meat—*senza carne*

I love you (to friends and family)—*ti voglio bene*

I love you (romantic)—*ti amo*

will you marry me?—*mi vuoi sposare?*

how delicious!—*buonissimo!*

can I have a little more? (and they will give you a mountain of food)—*potrei avere un altro po'?*

what a big fork you are! (complimenting your large appetite)—*che buona forchetta che sei!*

a thousand thanks—*grazie mille*

I would like some sorbet please—*vorrei un sorbetto, per favore*

could I have some coffee without milk?—*potrei avere un caffè senza latte?*

could I have some coffee with soy milk?—*potrei avere un caffè con latte di soia?*

could I have some coffee with almond milk?—*potrei avere un caffè con latte di mandorla?*

could I have some coffee with rice milk?—*potrei avere un caffè con latte di riso?*

MENU IDEAS

ALLERGEN-FREE ITALIAN (GLUTEN, SOY, AND NUT)

All vegan ingredients are dairy- and egg-free, which are two of the most common allergens among children and adults. Many of the recipes in this book can also be made gluten-free, soy-free, and nut-free by following the instructions.

If you are preparing a recipe for yourself or someone else with a food allergy, check all ingredient labels carefully to make sure that they are allergen-free. It is up to the consumer to avoid ingredients that contain allergens, allergen derivatives, or have been exposed to cross-contamination.

GLUTEN-FREE SUBSTITUTIONS

Flour: Bob's Red Mill Gluten-Free All-Purpose Baking Flour is an excellent product that can be substituted in many of my sweet and savory recipes calling for flour. It is made from a blend of garbanzo or chickpea flour and potato starch, and can be found at your local grocery store or ordered online at BobsRedMill.com. There are many brands of gluten-free flour, but I find the best results with Bob's Red Mill. When substituting gluten-free flour in a recipe, make sure that the other ingredients you are using in the recipe are gluten-free as well, such as pasta, bread products, seasonings, and so on.

Note that gluten-free flour can be used in almost all of my dessert recipes with excellent results, but it is very important to add xanthan gum (page 257) as directed in the recipe. Also, baking time may vary when using gluten-free flour.

Pasta: Any of my pasta recipes can be made using gluten-free noodles. Brown rice pasta is a delicious alternative to wheat pasta. You can substitute it in every one of my pasta recipes. Brown rice pasta takes longer to cook, so be sure to boil it until it is tender with a soft bite. You can also use quinoa pasta, which has a beautiful golden color.

Pizza: To make any of my pizza recipes gluten free, substitute my Gluten-Free Pizza Crust (page 235). It has a delicious flavor and cornmeal texture.

Bread: Gluten-free bread, often made from rice, flax, and almond flour, can be purchased at your local natural foods market and substituted in all recipes calling for bread. It is usually found in the freezer section of the grocery store. Use this to make gluten-free panini, sliders, or crostini.

Soy Sauce: Gluten-free tamari can be found at your local natural foods market and used in place of soy sauce. San-J is a popular brand that carries organic gluten-free soy sauce.

Seitan: For gluten-free cooking, avoid seitan, which is essentially made from pure wheat gluten. Instead, substitute extra-firm tofu or tempeh.

Bread crumbs: Use store-bought, gluten-free bread crumbs or make your own by toasting gluten-free bread and pulsing it in a food processor until the consistency is fine crumbs. Add a dash of Italian seasoning for Italian bread crumbs.

SOY-FREE SUBSTITUTIONS

Tofu and Tempeh: For soy-free cooking, avoid tofu or tempeh. In recipes that use pieces of tofu or tempeh, such as Baked Tempeh in Mushroom Cream Sauce (page 155) or Tempeh with 40 Cloves of Garlic (page 170), use seitan instead.

Cream Sauce: For a delicious soy-free cream sauce recipe, try my Bowties in Garlic Cream Sauce (page 121), which uses nuts, or my cauliflower Alfredo sauce (see Kate Middleton's Pasta Alfredo, page 116), which uses roasted cauliflower.

Margarine: Earth Balance is the leading brand of vegan margarine; it can be purchased in a soy-free variety.

NUT-FREE SUBSTITUTIONS

Nuts are used frequently in vegan cooking as cream and cheese substitutes, which can be problematic for those allergic to nuts. Luckily, in this book I use many other ingredients for cream and cheese substitutes.

Cream Sauce: For a delicious nut-free cream sauce recipe, try my carbonara sauce (see You-Won't-Be-Single-for-Long Pasta Carbonara with Shiitake Bacon, page 133), which uses tofu, or my cauliflower Alfredo sauce (see Kate Middleton's Pasta Alfredo, page 116), which uses roasted cauliflower.

Cheese substitute: For a nut-free cheese recipe, use my Rockin' Ricotta (page 242), which is made from tofu. Use this in place of the Mozzarella Sauce (page 237) or Parmesan Topping (page 244), which both contain nuts, for pizzas and pastas.

Pesto: Traditionally, pesto sauce is made with nuts, but if you are allergic, use instead my Quick Basil Pesto (see Mushroom Pesto Sliders, page 101), which is nut-free. This works great in my Pesto Mac 'n' Cheese (page 134), Grilled Pesto Pie (page 97), and any other recipe with pesto. If you want to make other pesto recipes nut-free, substitute pumpkin seeds for whichever nut is used.

APPETIZERS
(ANTIPASTI)

Sure, a platter of olives will do just fine as the appetizer for your next Italian dinner, but I'm raising the bar with some of my favorite wildly unique and interesting crostini, as well as some fusion starters like Pistachio Guacamole and Hummus Pomodoro.

FRIED ZUCCHINI
ZUCCHINE FRITTE

SERVES 6

Every culture has its french fry. Well, Italy is no exception, so behold this delicious, decadent, and slightly addictive appetizer!

1 cup all-purpose flour

2 teaspoons sea salt

1¼ cups soy, almond, or rice milk

Canola oil for frying

3 medium zucchini, trimmed and cut into 3 x ½-inch strips

½ cup Italian bread crumbs

In a medium bowl, whisk flour, salt, and nondairy milk.

Fill a large nonstick skillet with about ¼ inch oil and heat over medium-high heat. Dip zucchini in the batter, then roll in bread crumbs to coat. Fry on all sides until crisp and golden. Drain on paper towels and lightly season with more salt. Repeat with remaining zucchini and serve immediately.

CHERRY TOMATO BRUSCHETTA ON GRILLED BREAD
BRUSCHETTA DI POMODORO CILIEGINO

SERVES 6 TO 8

This classic bruschetta (pronounced bru-SKE-ta) can be paired with any recipe in this book for a knockout meal. A tablespoon of balsamic vinegar adds sweetness and brightens the flavor of the tomatoes.

1 pint cherry tomatoes, quartered

½ cup chopped fresh basil

1 tablespoon balsamic vinegar

1 tablespoon olive oil, plus extra for brushing

2 garlic cloves, crushed

½ teaspoon sea salt

½ teaspoon freshly ground black pepper

1 French baguette, cut into ½-inch slices on the diagonal

Preheat a grill or grill pan to high.

In a large bowl, toss tomatoes, basil, vinegar, 1 tablespoon oil, garlic, salt, and pepper. Set aside while flavors come together. Adjust seasoning to taste.

Brush bread slices with oil on both sides. Grill on both sides, until nice grill marks appear. Top with the tomato mixture and drizzle with oil.

EASY EGGPLANT CAPONATA
CAPONATA DI MELANZANE

SERVES 6 TO 8

I guarantee this recipe is easier and tastier than any other version you've tried. Traditionally, caponata is overcomplicated with added ingredients, but my version is quick and simple, highlighting the brilliant flavor of the eggplant.

MAKE-AHEAD TIP: Caponata can be made up to 3 days in advance and stored in the refrigerator.

Preheat the oven to 400°F.

Cut off the ends of the eggplant, then cut in half, lengthwise. Score the flesh of each half with a knife by making a few diagonal lines one way, then a few diagonal lines the other way. Cut deep into the flesh, but do not cut the skin. Lightly brush the flesh with oil and place, flat side down, on a large baking sheet. Roast for 40 minutes until flesh is soft. Let cool slightly.

Meanwhile, in a medium skillet, heat the 1 tablespoon oil over medium-high heat and add onion. Let cook until soft, then add tomato paste and let cook for 1 minute more. Stir in water and remove from heat.

Using a large spoon, scoop out the flesh of the eggplant and discard skins. Place the eggplant flesh in a food processor. Add the onion mixture, salt, red pepper, vinegar, cocoa, brown sugar, and capers. Pulse until almost combined but still slightly chunky. Transfer to a bowl, stir in mint to taste, and adjust seasoning to taste. Drizzle with oil and serve as a condiment on bread, crackers, or pita chips.

1 medium eggplant

1 tablespoon olive oil, plus extra for brushing and drizzling

1 onion, finely chopped

3 tablespoons tomato paste

¼ cup water

½ teaspoon sea salt

Pinch of crushed red pepper

1 tablespoon balsamic vinegar

1 teaspoon unsweetened cocoa powder

2 tablespoons brown sugar

2 tablespoons capers

1 to 2 tablespoons fresh mint, cut into chiffonade, see Tip (page 26)

Bread, crackers, or pita chips to serve

BAKED ITALIAN ONION RINGS
ANELLI DI CIPOLLA AL FORNO

SERVES 4

I actually hate onion rings. You know, the greasy kind you get at a twenty-four-hour burger joint? But these onion rings . . . Mmm! They are baked and expertly seasoned with Italian seasoning and a hint of chili pepper, which kicks them up a few notches.

MAKE-AHEAD TIP: After dipping onion rings in batter and dredging in bread crumb mixture, place on prepared baking sheet and cover with plastic wrap or foil. Store in refrigerator for up to 8 hours or overnight before baking.

2 cups Italian bread crumbs

2 teaspoons sea salt

1 teaspoon crushed red pepper (optional)

1 cup all-purpose flour

1¼ cups water

1 large onion, sliced into ½-inch rings

Olive oil for brushing

Arrabbiata sauce, for dipping (store-bought, or recipe on page 232)

Preheat the oven to 450°F. Generously grease one or two large baking sheets.

In a large bowl, combine bread crumbs, salt, and red pepper, if using. Mix thoroughly until combined, then divide the mixture into two small bowls and set aside.

In a medium bowl, whisk flour and water until a thick batter forms.

Separate onion rings. Dip each onion ring into the batter, letting any excess drip off. Using one of your bowls of bread crumbs first, dip the onion ring into the bread crumb mixture, coating completely, and place on prepared baking sheet. Repeat with remaining onion. About halfway through the process, when your bowl of bread crumb mixture gets too clumpy, discard the first bowl, and move on to the second bowl of bread crumb mixture.

Then, using a pastry brush, dab each onion ring with oil. Do this by dipping the brush in oil and patting each onion ring, rather than brushing. Bake for about 7 minutes until nicely golden, turn over each onion ring, and bake for 4 to 5 minutes more until golden. Season with salt and serve.

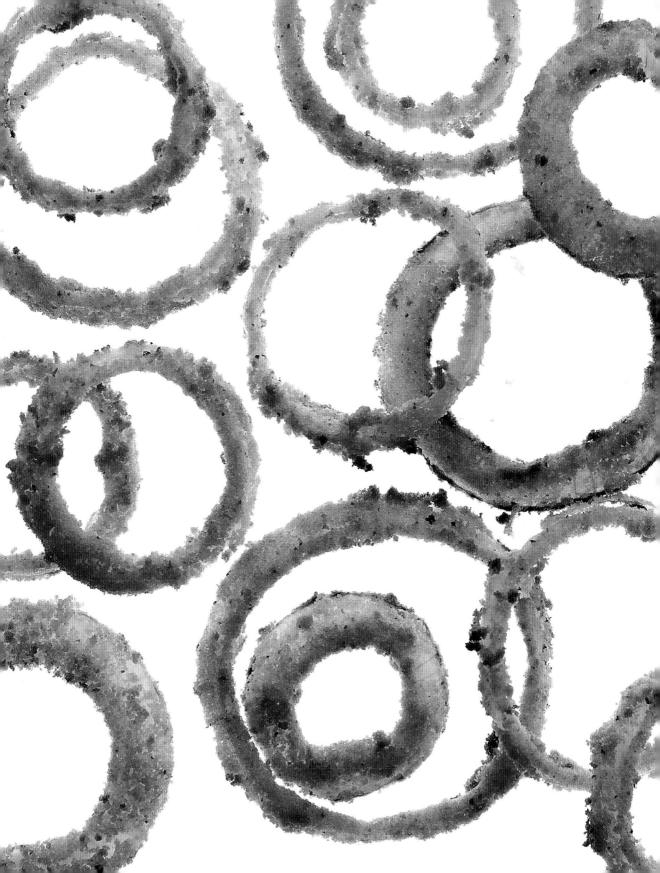

BUTTERNUT BRUSCHETTA WITH CARAMELIZED ONIONS

BRUSCHETTE ALLA ZUCCA CON CIPOLLE CARAMELLATE

SERVES 8 TO 10

Sweet roasted butternut squash mashed with caramelized onions schmeared on crostini will make you never look back on "regular" bruschetta. Drizzle it with balsamic vinegar or make a balsamic glaze by cooking it down to a syrupy consistency. I like it both ways!

MAKE-AHEAD TIP: The butternut squash topping can be made up to 3 days in advance and stored in the refrigerator.

4 cups (1-inch cubes) peeled butternut squash (about 20 ounces)

4 tablespoons olive oil

Sea salt

Freshly ground black pepper

2 large onions, thinly sliced

2 tablespoons maple syrup

¼ teaspoon crushed red pepper

2 teaspoons balsamic vinegar, plus extra for drizzling

1 thin baguette, cut into ¼-inch slices on the diagonal

¼ cup fresh mint, cut into chiffonade, see Tip (page 26)

Preheat the oven to 400°F.

Spread butternut squash on a large rimmed baking sheet and drizzle with 2 tablespoons of the oil. Season with salt and pepper. Let cook for 25 to 30 minutes until fork-tender. While roasting, turn with a spatula every 10 minutes and add more oil if needed. Remove from oven and increase heat to 425°F.

In a large skillet, heat the remaining 2 tablespoons oil over medium heat. Add onions and season with salt. Let cook until very soft and caramelized, 20 to 25 minutes. Add maple syrup and red pepper, and let cook for 1 minute more.

Combine squash, onion mixture, and vinegar in a food processor and pulse about 12 times until mixture comes together but is slightly chunky. Season to taste.

Place bread slices on a large baking sheet and drizzle with oil. Bake 5 to 8 minutes, or until lightly browned on top. Top bread with butternut squash mixture and drizzle with vinegar. Sprinkle with fresh mint and serve while warm.

CAPRESE SKEWERS

SPIEDINI ALLA CAPRESE

MAKES 24 BITE-SIZE SKEWERS

These are easy to make and even easier to pop into your mouth. This is a great appetizer to fool a nonvegan crowd because everyone thinks the tofu is mozzarella cheese. A lot of flavor is packed on a little skewer!

7 ounces extra-firm tofu, drained, patted dry with a paper towel, and cut into 1-inch cubes

1 tablespoon olive oil

½ teaspoon sea salt

¼ teaspoon freshly ground black pepper

½ cup cherry tomatoes, halved

¼ cup fresh basil, loosely packed

Balsamic vinegar for drizzling

In a large bowl, toss tofu, oil, salt, and pepper.

Heat a large nonstick skillet over medium-high heat and add tofu mixture. Sauté tofu cubes until all sides have been cooked and lightly browned.

Skewer 1 cube of tofu, 1 half cherry tomato, and 1 basil leaf on each toothpick or skewer. Drizzle with vinegar. Season with salt and pepper.

LA FAME E' IL MIGLIOR CONDIMENTO.

HUNGER IS THE BEST CONDIMENT.

HUMMUS POMODORO WITH WARM PIZZA CRUST *
HUMMUS DI POMODORO CON CROSTA DI PIZZA

SERVES 4 TO 6

I hum, you hum, we all hum for this hummus! Slather some creamy, garlicky white bean puree over hot and doughy pizza crust wedges topped with fresh tomato and basil . . . and then consider life complete.

For the hummus: Combine beans, oil, lemon juice, garlic, salt, and pepper in a food processor and process until smooth, stopping to scrape down the sides with a spatula. Adjust seasoning to taste and transfer to a bowl. Top with chopped tomato and basil, and drizzle with oil and vinegar. Season with salt and pepper and serve with warm pizza crust.

For the pizza crust: Preheat the oven to broil.

Divide dough into four equal pieces. Roll each piece into a ball and roll out on a lightly floured surface until about ⅛ inch thick. Place on a baking sheet, brush both sides with oil, and season with salt. Broil for 2 to 5 minutes until lightly browned, then flip using tongs, and broil for another 1 to 2 minutes, or until puffed and lightly browned in spots. Cut into triangles and serve warm with hummus.

HUMMUS

1 can white beans, rinsed and drained

¼ cup olive oil, plus extra for drizzling

1 tablespoon lemon juice

1 garlic clove

½ teaspoon sea salt

½ teaspoon freshly ground black pepper

1 medium tomato, chopped

¼ cup fresh chopped basil

Balsamic vinegar for drizzling

PIZZA CRUST

1 pound pizza dough

All-purpose flour for rolling

Olive oil for brushing

Sea salt

ITALIAN QUESADILLAS*
QUESADILLAS ALL'ITALIANA

SERVES 10 TO 12 AS AN APPETIZER; 4 AS A MEAL

I know, I know, you're probably thinking, "Chloe, what the heck are you doing putting quesadillas in an Italian cookbook?" Try these and I promise you will thank me! Kids and adults love these comforting and creamy white bean quesadillas stuffed with avocado, herbs, and sweet sun-dried tomatoes. Chicken quesadillas, get out of town!

MAKE-AHEAD TIP: White bean spread can be made up to 3 days in advance and stored in the refrigerator.

WHITE BEAN SPREAD

1 (15-ounce) can white beans, rinsed and drained

¼ cup olive oil, plus extra for brushing

1 tablespoon water

1 tablespoon lemon juice

1 garlic clove

¾ teaspoon sea salt

½ teaspoon freshly ground black pepper

8 flour tortillas

½ cup chopped sun-dried tomatoes, drained

¼ cup chopped fresh Italian parsley

2 avocados, very thinly sliced

For the white bean spread: Combine beans, oil, water, lemon juice, garlic, salt, and pepper in a food processor and process until smooth. Add more salt to taste. Set aside.

To assemble the quesadillas: Spread about 5 tablespoons of white bean spread on a tortilla, leaving a ½-inch border. Arrange 2 tablespoons sun-dried tomatoes, 1 tablespoon parsley, and avocado on top of the spread. Season with salt and pepper and place another tortilla on top. Brush both sides of the quesadilla with oil.

Heat a large nonstick skillet over medium-high heat and cook the quesadilla about 2 minutes on each side, until lightly browned. Remove from pan and slice like a pizza to serve. Repeat assembly and cooking method with remaining ingredients, making a total of 4 quesadillas.

PARMESAN PITA CRISPS
PITA FRITTA AL PARMIGIANO

SERVES 6

Some people say these crispy, cheesy dippers remind them of Doritos, others say they taste like Parmesan. Luckily, they are much healthier than either. I usually serve these with my Lemony Chickpea Puree (below) or Pistachio Guacamole (page 22).

10 ounces pita pockets, sliced into small triangles

¼ cup olive oil, plus more as needed

1 teaspoon sea salt

1 tablespoon nutritional yeast flakes

Preheat the oven to 400°F.

In a large bowl toss pita triangles with oil and salt. Add more oil as needed until each piece is coated on both sides. Spread on a large rimmed baking sheet and sprinkle evenly with nutritional yeast. Bake for 10 to 15 minutes, until lightly browned and crisp, tossing the pita chips with a spatula halfway through baking. Let cool on the baking sheet.

LEMONY CHICKPEA PUREE
PURÈ DI CÉCE AL LIMONE

SERVES 6

The chickpea is a popular bean in Italian cuisine. This recipe is an elevated take on hummus, packed with extra flavor from lemon and capers.

1 can chickpeas, rinsed and drained

¼ cup olive oil

2 tablespoons, plus 1 teaspoon lemon juice

2 tablespoons capers

¼ teaspoon cayenne

½ teaspoon sea salt

½ teaspoon freshly ground black pepper

Parmesan Pita Crisps (above)

Combine all ingredients in food processor and process until smooth, stopping to scrape down the sides with a spatula. Season to taste and serve with Parmesan pita crisps.

MUSHROOM PESTO CROSTINI
CROSTINI AL PESTO DI FUNGHI

SERVES 4 TO 6

Mushrooms give this pesto a hearty and earthy flavor that makes this the ultimate savory crostini.

Preheat the oven to 425°F.

Heat oil in a large nonstick skillet over medium-high heat and cook mushrooms and onion until soft and lightly browned. Add garlic and cook a few more minutes.

Meanwhile, in a food processor, add walnuts and process until a fine meal is formed. Add mushroom mixture, lemon juice, salt, pepper, red pepper, and parsley. Pulse just until the mixture is combined, but still has some texture.

Place bread slices on a large baking sheet and drizzle with oil. Bake 5 to 8 minutes, or until lightly browned on top.

Top each crostini with mushroom pesto. Very lightly drizzle with oil and season with salt, if desired. Garnish with parsley and serve.

2 tablespoons olive oil, plus more for drizzling

1 pound mixed mushrooms, trimmed and sliced

1 onion, chopped

2 garlic cloves, minced

1 cup walnuts

1 tablespoon lemon juice

1 teaspoon sea salt

1 teaspoon freshly ground black pepper

¼ teaspoon crushed red pepper

1 cup fresh Italian parsley, plus extra for garnish

1 thin baguette, cut into ¼-inch slices on the diagonal

ASPARAGI E FUNGHI INSEGNANO L'UMILTÀ AL CUOCO.

(ASPARAGUS AND MUSHROOMS TEACH A COOK HUMILITY.)

PISTACHIO GUACAMOLE*
GUACAMOLE AL PISTACCHIO

SERVES 4

Holy Italian Guacamole! Pureed pistachios add extra creaminess to avocados mashed with garlic, scallions, and cherry tomatoes. Just watch the faces of your friends and family as they dig in and declare they'll never eat plain guacamole again! Serve with store-bought chips or, if you want to make your own dipper, try my Crostini (page 235), Parmesan Pita Crisps (page 20), or Warm Pizza Crust (page 17).

2 avocados

½ cup shelled pistachios, plus extra for garnish

2 tablespoons lemon juice

2 tablespoons water

1 garlic clove, minced

¾ teaspoon sea salt

Freshly ground black pepper

1 cup cherry tomatoes, quartered

1 bunch (about 6) scallions, white and light green parts thinly sliced

Crushed red pepper for serving

Chips for serving

Place one of the avocados, pistachios, lemon juice, water, garlic, and salt in a food processor. Season generously with pepper and process until smooth. Transfer to a large bowl and mash in the remaining avocado, so the texture is chunky. Fold in tomatoes and scallions. Adjust seasoning to taste. Sprinkle with red pepper and top with pistachios.

SMASHED AVOCADO AND ROASTED BEET CROSTINI

CROSTINI CON BARBABIETOLE ARROSTITE ED AVOCADO

SERVES 6 TO 8

Try serving this appetizer to a beet hater and watch him fall in love. It's fun!

Preheat the oven to 425°F. Line a baking sheet with foil.

Arrange beets on prepared baking sheet and toss with oil. Season with salt and roast for 30 minutes, turning occasionally with a spatula. Remove pan from oven, drizzle with maple syrup and vinegar, return to oven, and roast for 5 to 8 minutes until caramelized.

Place bread slices on another large baking sheet and drizzle with oil. Bake for 5 to 8 minutes, or until lightly browned on top.

In a small bowl, mash avocado and juice from half of the lemon with a fork. Season with salt and pepper.

Spread a thin layer of mashed avocado on each crostini. Top with roasted beets, season with pepper, and drizzle with the remaining lemon juice.

2 beets (about 1 pound), peeled and chopped into ½-inch pieces

2 tablespoons olive oil, plus extra for brushing

Sea salt

2 tablespoons maple syrup

1 tablespoon balsamic vinegar

½ baguette, cut into ¼-inch slices on the diagonal

1 avocado

1 lemon, halved

Freshly ground black pepper

WHITE BEAN CROSTINI WITH POMEGRANATE AND MINT*

CROSTINI AI FAGIOLI BIANCHI E MELOGRANO CON PROFUMO DI MENTA

SERVES 6 TO 8

Praise the Italian lord for white beans! They're high in protein, low in fat, and deliciously savory and creamy when pureed. The pomegranate and mint add a pop of freshness and make this crostini festive around Christmas.

1 (15-ounce) can white beans, rinsed and drained

¼ cup olive oil, plus extra for brushing

1 tablespoon water

1 tablespoon lemon juice

1 garlic clove

¾ teaspoon sea salt

½ teaspoon freshly ground black pepper

1 thin baguette, cut into ¼-inch slices on the diagonal

¼ cup pomegranate seeds

Fresh mint for garnish, cut into chiffonade, see Tip

For the white bean puree: Combine beans, oil, water, lemon juice, garlic, salt, and pepper in a food processor and process until smooth. Add more salt to taste. Set aside.

For the crostini: Preheat the oven to 425°F.

Place bread slices on a large baking sheet and drizzle with oil. Bake for 5 to 8 minutes, or until lightly browned on top.

Spread a thin layer of white bean puree on each crostini. Top with pomegranate seeds and mint.

CHLOE'S TIP: CHIFFONADE

Chiffonade means "made of rags." To cut an herb or leafy vegetable in chiffonade, first stack the leaves as evenly as you can. Roll the stack tightly so it resembles a cigar. Slice the roll crosswise into very thin slices, and pull apart the slices into strips. A chiffonade of basil or mint is used quite often as a garnish.

RED AND YELLOW PEPPER CROSTINI
CROSTINI AI PEPERONI

SERVES 4 TO 6

The key to this dish is cooking down the peppers for a full half hour until they are super soft and caramelized. Plan a distraction while they cook and be patient—the reward will be sweet!

2 tablespoons olive oil, plus extra for drizzling

3 large bell peppers (red, yellow, and orange), thinly sliced

1 teaspoon sea salt

Freshly ground black pepper

1 thin baguette, cut into ¼-inch slices on the diagonal

Preheat the oven to 425°F.

In a large skillet, heat the oil over medium heat and add bell peppers and salt. Season with pepper. Let cook, stirring occasionally, until very soft (about 30 minutes). Adjust seasoning to taste.

Meanwhile, place bread slices on a large baking sheet and drizzle with oil. Bake for 5 to 8 minutes, or until lightly browned on top.

Top each crostini with bell peppers and serve.

HERBED RISOTTO CAKES WITH ARRABBIATA DIPPING SAUCE

TORTINE DI RISOTTO ALL'ARRABBIATA

MAKES ABOUT 12 (2-INCH) CAKES

Every time I host a dinner party with these on the menu, they are the standout hit of the night. The cakes have a crispy salty exterior with creamy cheesy risotto on the inside, all dipped in a spicy arrabbiata sauce. Arrabbiata means "angry" in Italian, so the sauce gets its name from the heat of the chili peppers. Cute, huh?

MAKE-AHEAD TIP: Risotto cakes can be formed and frozen. Thaw overnight in refrigerator and panfry before serving.

For the risotto cakes: In a large pot, bring rice, water, and 1 teaspoon of the salt to a boil. Reduce heat to medium and simmer, uncovered, for about 20 minutes, stirring occasionally. Transfer to a large colander or strainer, rinse with cold water, and drain well.

In a large bowl, add the rice, nutritional yeast, the remaining 1¼ teaspoons salt, pepper, and Italian seasoning, and mix well with a large spoon. Using your hands, form rice mixture into 2-inch patties. Place bread crumbs on a plate and coat patties with bread crumbs.

In a large nonstick skillet, heat oil over medium-high heat and panfry patties. Let cook until lightly browned and crisp on both sides. Repeat with remaining patties, adding more oil if needed. Serve immediately with warm arrabbiata sauce for dipping.

1¼ cups uncooked Arborio rice

8 cups water

2¼ teaspoons sea salt

¼ cup nutritional yeast flakes

½ teaspoon freshly ground black pepper

1 teaspoon Italian seasoning

½ cup Italian bread crumbs

2 tablespoons olive oil

Arrabbiata sauce for dipping (store-bought or recipe on page 232)

VEGETABLES
(VERDURE)

Italians do vegetables best—simply prepared using olive oil, salt, and pepper. I tried to stick to tradition, but couldn't help myself from adding in an occasional pomegranate reduction or cashew cream.

ROASTED CAULIFLOWER WITH ONION, GARLIC, AND THYME

CAVOLFIORE ARROSTITO CON CIPOLLA, AGLIO, E TIMO

SERVES 4

I love this simple side dish because it pairs well with just about anything in this book. It's pleasantly aromatic, making it the perfect subtle vegetable for an entrée that screams for attention.

NOTE: For a shortcut, purchase precut cauliflower at the grocery store.

MAKE-AHEAD TIP: Cauliflower can be roasted a day in advance and kept refrigerated. Reheat before serving.

1 small head cauliflower, cut into florets

1 onion, sliced

4 garlic cloves, unpeeled

6 sprigs fresh thyme

4 tablespoons olive oil

Sea salt

Freshly ground black pepper

Preheat the oven to 400°F.

Spread cauliflower, onion, garlic, and thyme in one layer on a large rimmed baking sheet and drizzle with oil. Season with salt and pepper.

Roast for 35 to 45 minutes, or until fork-tender, stirring frequently with a spatula or large spoon to even out the browning. Taste occasionally to see if more salt or pepper is needed. Remove from oven, remove garlic cloves, and season to taste.

ARTICHOKE HASH BROWNS*
FRITTELLE DI PATATE CON CARCIOFI

SERVES 4

Everyone loves hash browns, but I love adding artichokes, garlic, and crushed red pepper for some Italian flavor. Using frozen shredded hash browns makes for a super-duper crispy, potatoey, salty, okeydokey-artichokey quick fix!

3 tablespoons olive oil

1 (14-ounce) can artichoke hearts, drained and sliced

2 garlic cloves, crushed

⅛ teaspoon crushed red pepper

1 pound frozen hash browns

Sea salt

Freshly ground black pepper

In a large nonstick skillet, heat 1 tablespoon of the oil over medium heat. Sauté artichoke hearts, garlic, and red pepper for a few minutes until fragrant. Add frozen (shredded, un-thawed) hash browns and season with salt and pepper. Add the remaining 2 tablespoons oil. Let cook on medium-high heat until hash browns get golden brown and crispy, turning occasionally with a spatula. Add more oil as needed and season to taste with salt and pepper.

BALSAMIC GRILLED ZUCCHINI
ZUCCHINE GRIGLIATE CON ACETO BALSAMICO

SERVES 4

I first tried this dish while visiting Italian friends in a small town called Lecce. My nonna (grand-mother), Lina, cooked an Italian feast and made a whole separate vegan menu just for me! This was one of my favorite vegetable dishes, so I begged for the recipe. Turns out, it's really simple. I prefer to use aged balsamic vinegar for a sweeter flavor.

2 zucchini, thinly sliced lengthwise (about ¼ inch thick)

Olive oil for brushing

Sea salt

Freshly ground black pepper

Balsamic vinegar for drizzling

Preheat a grill or grill pan.

Brush zucchini with oil on both sides and season with salt and pepper. Grill until tender and nice grill marks appear. Be sure to flip and cook each side.

Transfer to a plate and drizzle with vinegar.

Artichoke Hash Browns
(recipe on opposite page)

ROASTED POTATOES WITH GREMOLATA*
PATATE ARROSTITE CON LA GREMOLADA

SERVES 4

Gremolata is an Italian topping made of crushed garlic, parsley, olive oil, and lemon zest. It's commonly served on meat and fish, but wouldn't you rather have it on crispy roasted potatoes? Yes, please!

ROASTED POTATOES

1¼ pounds new potatoes, cut into bite-size pieces

3 tablespoons olive oil

¾ teaspoon sea salt

GREMOLATA

¼ cup chopped fresh Italian parsley

2 garlic cloves, finely minced or crushed

Zest of 1 lemon

1 tablespoon olive oil

¼ teaspoon sea salt

¼ teaspoon freshly ground black pepper

For the roasted potatoes: Preheat the oven to 400°F.

Spread the potatoes on a large rimmed baking sheet and drizzle with oil and season with salt. Toss with a spatula to coat. Roast for 35 to 45 minutes, or until fork-tender and crisp, turning once or twice with a spatula to ensure even browning.

For the gremolata: Combine all the ingredients in a small bowl. Mash with a mortar and pestle or the back of a spoon until well combined.

In a large bowl, toss roasted potatoes with the gremolata. Add more salt to taste and serve.

GARLIC FIRE-ROASTED CORN
MAIS ARROSTITO CON AGLIO

SERVES 4

If you love garlic and you love corn, this is for you. It's a nice way to punch up a summer favorite and it cooks up quickly right on top of your stovetop gas burner. There's nothing like that pop of yellow on your picnic table.

In a small saucepan, whisk oil and garlic over medium heat until fragrant. Set aside.

Using tongs, place ears of corn directly on the open flame of a stovetop gas burner or grill and roast, turning frequently to make sure all sides are cooked and lightly charred. Once each corn is completely cooked, remove from heat.

Brush corn with oil mixture, sprinkle with parsley, and drizzle with lemon juice. Season with salt and serve warm.

¼ cup olive oil

2 garlic cloves, minced or crushed

4 ears of corn, silk removed

1 tablespoon finely chopped parsley

1 lemon, halved

Sea salt

AGGIUNGI PEPE, SALE
E UN PIZZICO D'AMORE.

(IN MAKING DINNER FOR A FRIEND, DON'T FORGET THE LOVE.)

LEMONADE CAULIFLOWER *
CAVOLFIORE ALLA LIMONATA

SERVES 2

This roasted cauliflower really packs a punch with a sweet maple drizzle and tangy lemon zest, just like a glass of tangy lemonade! Tell picky veggie eaters the name of this dish and they're sure to take a bite. This recipe can be easily doubled to serve more people.

NOTE: For a shortcut, purchase precut cauliflower florets at the grocery store.

MAKE-AHEAD TIP: Cauliflower can be roasted a day in advance and kept refrigerated. Reheat before serving.

12 ounces cauliflower florets, not frozen

Olive oil

Sea salt

Freshly ground black pepper

1 teaspoon maple syrup

Zest of 1 lemon

Preheat the oven to 400°F.

Spread cauliflower in one layer on a large rimmed baking sheet and drizzle with oil. Season with salt and pepper.

Roast for 30 minutes, stirring once with a spatula or large spoon to even out the browning. Remove from oven, drizzle with maple syrup, and return to oven to roast for about 10 minutes, or until nicely browned and fork-tender. Remove from oven, toss with lemon zest, and season to taste.

UN CONTORNO ADATTO FARA' ONORE AL PIATTO.

(THE RIGHT SIDE DISH WILL BRING HONOR TO YOUR PLATE.)

BRAISED KALE WITH PINE NUTS AND CRANBERRIES

CAVOLO RICCIO BRASATO CON PINOLI E MIRTILLI ROSSI

SERVES 3

This is my favorite way to eat kale. It's amazing served hot or cold. A splash of lemon juice at the end adds flavor, but remember to never add lemon juice to greens while they are cooking in the pan because the acid will turn them brown. All hail kale!

In a large skillet, heat oil and garlic clove over medium heat. Add kale and season with salt and pepper. Let cook until almost wilted, tossing frequently. Add pine nuts and cranberries and cook for 1 minute more. Add vegetable broth and let cook until the kale softens and the broth evaporates. Remove from heat, remove garlic clove, and transfer kale to a plate. Drizzle with lemon juice before serving and season to taste.

2 tablespoons olive oil

1 garlic clove, peeled and smashed

½ bunch curly kale, cut into a chiffonade, see Tip (page 26), or torn into pieces

Sea salt

Freshly ground black pepper

2 tablespoons pine nuts

¼ cup dried cranberries

½ cup vegetable broth

Half a lemon

EGGPLANT ALLA FUNGHETTO
MELANZANE A FUNGHETTO

SERVES 6

My best friend, Danielle, introduced me to this dish in Italy. You may think this is a mushroom dish with a word like "funghetto" in the title, but it's not! Essentially it means eggplant (melanzane) cooked in the style of little mushrooms (funghetto). The eggplant is cut into bite-size pieces and sautéed until very soft with tomatoes, garlic, and sea salt. I ordered it once at a restaurant in New York City and it wasn't the same, so Danielle brought me this special recipe from Italy, and it just happens to be vegan. Grazie!

Serve over brown rice or quinoa, as a cold vegetable salad, or on crostini or bruschetta.

3 tablespoons olive oil

3 garlic cloves, peeled and smashed

1 large eggplant, unpeeled and cut into ½-inch pieces

1 large tomato, chopped

¾ teaspoon sea salt

Freshly ground black pepper

2 tablespoons chopped fresh Italian parsley

In a large skillet, heat oil over medium-high heat and add garlic cloves. Let cook for 2 minutes until fragrant. Add eggplant and tomato and cook until browned, about 15 minutes. Carefully add water, 1 tablespoon at a time, if eggplant sticks to the pan. Add salt and season with pepper. Cook until eggplant is very soft. Adjust seasoning to taste and remove garlic cloves. Top with parsley and serve.

PARMESAN ROASTED ASPARAGUS *

ASPARAGI ARROSTITI AL PARMIGIANO

SERVES 4

This is hands down my favorite vegetable recipe in the ~~book~~ universe! People mmm and aah at my dinner table when I serve it, and everyone asks how the heck there's no cheese in it. Just trust me—impress your mom, friend, or amore with this dish and you'll be considered a master chef forever.

Preheat the oven to 400°F.

On a large rimmed baking sheet, toss asparagus with enough oil to coat and season with salt and pepper.

Roast for 12 to 18 minutes until fork-tender and tips are slightly crispy. Remove from oven and season to taste. Very lightly squeeze lemon juice over asparagus and sprinkle with 1 to 2 tablespoons of Parmesan topping.

1 bunch asparagus, ends trimmed

2 tablespoons olive oil

Sea salt

Freshly ground black pepper

Half a lemon

Parmesan Topping (page 244)

CHLOE'S TIP: ASPARAGUS

Keep the grocery store rubber bands on the bunch of asparagus while you trim the ends. This way, they will stay put on your cutting board.

POMEGRANATE ROASTED BRUSSELS SPROUTS*
CAVOLETTI DI BRUXELLES ARROSTITI AL MELOGRANO

SERVES 6 TO 8

The combination of tangy pomegranate juice and sweet caramelized Brussels sprouts is finger-licking decadent. I have been known to stand over the oven after taking these out and eating half the tray before it reaches the dinner table. If you hate Brussels sprouts, I beg you to try these— you'll want more.

1½ pounds Brussels sprouts

¼ cup olive oil

¾ teaspoon sea salt

¼ teaspoon freshly ground black pepper

½ cup pure pomegranate juice

1 tablespoon maple syrup

¼ cup sliced almonds, toasted

Preheat the oven to 375°F.

To prepare Brussels sprouts, remove any yellow or brown outer leaves, cut off the stems, and cut in halves or quarters. On a large rimmed baking sheet, toss Brussels sprouts with oil, salt, and pepper until thoroughly coated.

Roast Brussels sprouts for 30 to 40 minutes, depending on the size of the Brussels sprouts. Check every 10 minutes, turning frequently with a spatula to ensure even roasting, until Brussels sprouts are fork-tender.

Meanwhile, in a small saucepan, cook and stir pomegranate juice and maple syrup over medium heat until it comes to a simmer. Let simmer, uncovered, for 10 to 15 minutes, or until it reduces to a syrup-like consistency.

Drizzle the roasted Brussels sprouts with pomegranate syrup and toss with almonds.

CHILI LEMON BROCCOLI
BROCCOLI AL LIMONE E PEPERONCINO

SERVES 4

This is my dad's favorite way to eat broccoli, and we always fight over the last piece. It's about the easiest way to prepare broccoli, but it is tangy and flavorful—perfect for a quick weeknight vegetable.

1 head broccoli, cut into florets

Olive oil

Sea salt

Freshly ground black pepper

Crushed red pepper

Half a lemon

Steam or boil broccoli until very soft and fork-tender. Arrange on a platter and drizzle with oil. Season with salt and pepper, then sprinkle with red pepper. Drizzle with lemon juice.

MASHED POTATOES WITH GARLIC AND SEA SALT
PURÈ DI PATATE CON AGLIO E SALE MARINO

SERVES 4

Need a hug or someone to comfort you? Try a bowl of these mashers instead! It'll do the trick.

2 russet potatoes, peeled and cut into 2-inch pieces

¾ cup vegetable broth, or soy, almond, coconut, or rice milk

2 garlic cloves, crushed

2 tablespoons olive oil

Sea salt

Freshly ground black pepper

Place potatoes in a large pot and cover with cold water. Generously salt the water, cover, and bring to a boil. Boil until potatoes are fork-tender. Drain and return to the pot.

Add broth, garlic, and oil, and mash. Season with salt and pepper and add more broth or oil as needed.

BROCCOLI RABE WITH GARLICKY BREAD BITES
RAPE CON BOCCONCINI DI PANE ALL'AGLIO

SERVES 4 TO 6

As a kid, I hated broccoli rabe. "It's so bitter! Why must we submit ourselves to such torture?" Then my mom created this recipe, and I'm obsessed! The bread bites soak up the moisture and flavor of the olive oil and garlic, which lessens the bitterness of broccoli rabe and makes for an ultra-savory side dish.

Remove any wilted or yellow leaves from the broccoli rabe and trim the bottom stems that are tough and thick. Rinse the broccoli rabe well and cut into 3-inch pieces. You will use the entire bunch, leaves too.

Bring a large pot of salted water to a boil. Add broccoli rabe and let cook for 3 to 5 minutes, or until desired tenderness. Drain in a colander. While broccoli is in the colander, heat oil over medium-high heat in the same pot and add bread cubes. Cook, turning frequently, until they begin to turn golden, about 5 minutes. Add garlic, red pepper, and broccoli rabe. Season with salt and pepper, and let cook a few more minutes. If needed, add more oil. Bread bites should turn soft. Season to taste and serve.

2 bunches broccoli rabe

2 tablespoons olive oil

2 cups (1-inch) bread cubes

2 garlic cloves, minced

¼ teaspoon crushed red pepper

Sea salt

Freshly ground black pepper

CREAMED SPINACH

VELLUTATA DI SPINACI

SERVES 3 TO 4

This is a new, modern vegan approach to the classic creamed spinach we've eaten at weddings and Thanksgiving tables. This updated version is less rich and much creamier, with a lovely garlicky flavor.

½ cup raw cashews*

½ cup water

1 tablespoon olive oil

1 small onion, finely chopped

10 ounces baby spinach

3 garlic cloves, minced

¾ teaspoon sea salt

Freshly ground black pepper

Pinch of ground nutmeg

*If you are not using a high-powered blender, such as a Vitamix, soak cashews overnight or boil cashews for 10 minutes and drain. This will soften the cashews and ensure a silky smooth cream.

Combine cashews and water in a blender and process for at least 1 minute on high speed until very smooth. Set aside.

In a large skillet, heat oil over medium-high and add onion. Cook until soft. Add spinach and let cook until wilted, about 5 minutes. Add garlic and cook for for 1 minute, until fragrant. Add cashew cream, and let cook a few more minutes until heated through. Season with salt, pepper, and nutmeg to taste and serve warm.

ROSEMARY SWEET POTATOES WITH SWEET 'N' SPICY MUSTARD *
PATATE DOLCI AL ROSMARINO CON SENAPE PICCANTE

SERVES 4 TO 6

I love sweet potatoes so much that I almost turned into one! When I was a baby I was rushed to the hospital; my skin turned orange from too much beta-carotene because I'd eaten so many sweet potatoes. In this dish, I roast them until sweet and crispy with sea salt and rosemary, and then dip them in a sweet-and-spicy mustard sauce. Use toothpicks if serving this to a large crowd for easy eating.

Preheat the oven to 400°F.

In a large bowl, toss sweet potatoes with enough oil to coat. Add rosemary and salt and toss again. Season with pepper.

Spread sweet potatoes on a large rimmed baking sheet. Roast for 30 to 40 minutes until fork-tender, stirring frequently with a spatula or large spoon to even out the browning. Remove from oven and adjust seasoning to taste.

1½ to 2 pounds sweet potatoes, unpeeled and cut into bite-size pieces

¼ cup olive oil, plus more as needed

1 tablespoon chopped fresh rosemary

1 teaspoon sea salt

Freshly ground black pepper

MUSTARD DIPPING SAUCE

In a small bowl, whisk mustard and brown sugar thoroughly until combined and sugar is dissolved. Serve with sweet potatoes.

⅓ cup yellow, spicy brown, or whole grain mustard

⅓ cup brown sugar

Avocado Caprese Pasta Salad
(recipe on page 56)

SOUPS AND SALADS

(ZUPPA E INSALATA)

My Italian-style soups and salads reach far beyond the expected minestrone or insalata mista that every vegan can order in an Italian restaurant. Instead, I use Italian ingredients such as fennel, grapefruit, tomato, and basil. You'll see that some recipes are classically inspired, like panzanella (bread salad) and some are vegan inspired, like cream of mushroom soup with fresh Italian parsley.

AVOCADO CAPRESE PASTA SALAD*

INSALATA DI PASTA ALLA CAPRESE CON AVOCADO

SERVES 6

This beautiful, fresh summer pasta salad (see the accompanying photo on page 54) is one of my favorites. The avocado adds creaminess and replaces mozzarella, which is traditionally found in caprese salad. I like using whole wheat fusilli because it adds a toothsome bite and catches the creamy avocado in its ridges.

1 pound whole wheat fusilli (or gluten-free pasta)

2 tablespoons olive oil, plus more as needed

2 tablespoons lemon juice

2 garlic cloves, minced

2 teaspoons sea salt

½ teaspoon crushed red pepper

2 cups cherry tomatoes, halved

1 cup basil, cut into chiffonade, see Tip (page 26)

2 ripe avocados, cut into small cubes

Freshly ground black pepper

Bring a large pot of salted water to a boil. Add fusilli and cook according to package directions. Drain, rinse with cold water, and return to the pot. Toss noodles with oil and set aside.

Add lemon juice, garlic, salt, red pepper, tomatoes, basil, and avocado. Season with black pepper. Wearing gloves, toss noodles with your hands, mashing the avocado slightly with your fingers. Drizzle more oil as needed, and season to taste.

PASTA AND BEANS
PASTA AI FAGIOLI

SERVES 6

My version of this Italian staple is easy, easy, easy! I find many recipes for pasta and beans over-complicated, so this is my no-nonsense, deliciously simple, one-pot way of doing it. The concept of pasta and beans originated as a poor person's stew of leftover pasta sauce, but now it is served at the finest Italian restaurants.

NOTE: If served immediately, this dish is more like a soup. It will thicken as it sits. I like it both ways!

In a large pot, heat oil over medium-high heat and add onion and carrot. Cook until soft, then add garlic and let cook for 1 minute more, until fragrant. Add broth, water, tomato sauce, beans, thyme, salt, and pepper. Let cook, uncovered, until liquid begins to boil. Add pasta and let boil gently, stirring frequently, until pasta is tender. Add salt to taste and serve.

2 tablespoons olive oil

1 small onion, finely chopped

1 carrot, peeled and finely chopped

2 garlic cloves, minced

3 cups vegetable broth

1 cup water

1 (8-ounce) can tomato sauce

1 (15-ounce) can cannellini beans, rinsed and drained

1 tablespoon fresh thyme leaves

1 teaspoon sea salt

½ teaspoon freshly ground black pepper

¾ cup small pasta shells or tubes (or gluten-free pasta)

ARTICHOKE PESTO PASTA SALAD

INSALATA DI PASTA AL PESTO DI CARCIOFI

SERVES 4 TO 6

This tangy pasta salad is perfect for any artichoke or pesto lover. You could also serve it as a hot pasta dish if desired. You can use any pasta shape, but I love orecchiette (or "little ears") because it catches the pesto so perfectly.

MAKE-AHEAD TIP: This pasta is best made just before serving. After 24 hours, it will still taste great, but the color will start to darken.

1 pound orecchiette (or gluten-free pasta)

1 (14-ounce) can artichoke hearts, drained (can also use marinated or frozen and thawed)

1 cup packed fresh Italian parsley

¾ cup walnuts

1 garlic clove

1 tablespoon lemon juice

1¼ teaspoons sea salt

1 teaspoon freshly ground black pepper

½ cup olive oil

½ cup water

Bring a large pot of salted water to a boil. Add orecchiette and cook according to package directions. Drain, rinse with cold water, and return to the pot.

In a food processor, pulse artichoke hearts, parsley, walnuts, garlic, lemon juice, salt, pepper, oil, and water until combined. Do not overprocess; leave a bit of texture to the sauce.

Toss pasta with sauce and season to taste.

SWEET POTATO AND ALMOND COUSCOUS SALAD
INSALATA DI COUSCOUS CON PATATE DOLCI E MANDORLE

SERVES 4 TO 6

Hug, hug, cous, cous! Everyone will be friendly at your dinner party after a serving of this wildly flavorful couscous salad—chock-full of roasted sweet potatoes, fresh orange juice and zest, cranberries, and fresh thyme.

MAKE-AHEAD TIP: Entire recipe (minus the fresh thyme) can be made the day before serving and stored in the refrigerator. Toss with fresh thyme before serving.

Preheat the oven to 375°F.

In a large bowl, toss 2 tablespoons of the oil with potatoes and season with salt and pepper to taste. Transfer to a large rimmed baking sheet and roast for 40 to 45 minutes until fork-tender, turning once or twice with a spatula. Let cool.

In the meantime, combine the 1 tablespoon oil, couscous, the 1 teaspoon salt, and broth in a medium saucepan. Bring to a boil; reduce heat and simmer, covered, for 10 minutes until tender. Remove from heat and let sit, covered, for 5 minutes, or until all liquid has been absorbed. Toss couscous with the remaining 1 tablespoon oil and spread on a large rimmed baking sheet to cool.

Toss cooled couscous with roasted sweet potato, orange zest and juice, cranberries, almonds, and thyme. Season to taste and serve.

4 tablespoons olive oil

2 large sweet potatoes, peeled and cut into ½-inch cubes

1 teaspoon sea salt, plus more to taste

Freshly ground black pepper

2 cups Israeli pearl couscous

2½ cups vegetable broth

Zest and juice of 1 orange

¼ cup dried cranberries

¼ cup sliced or slivered almonds, toasted

2 tablespoons fresh thyme leaves

GRAPEFRUIT, AVOCADO, AND FENNEL SALAD
INSALATA DI POMPELMO, AVOCADO, E FINOCCHIO

SERVES 4

This title may sound like a picky eater's worst nightmare, but the overall flavor is surprisingly pleasant. The sweet and sour grapefruit with the mild and creamy avocado tossed with crispy fennel makes the perfect side salad for any meal.

This light and fresh California-style salad is the perfect complement to a hearty pasta. The sweet agave vinaigrette softens the peppery flavor of the arugula, and the grapefruit adds a refreshing burst of citrus.

2 large grapefruit, segmented and juice reserved, see Tip (opposite page)

1 tablespoon olive oil

2 tablespoons apple cider vinegar

1 tablespoon agave

3 cups baby arugula

1 small fennel bulb, shaved as thinly as possible, see Tip below

1 avocado, sliced

Sea salt and freshly ground black pepper

Segment the grapefruit, and squeeze remaining juice from the membrane. You'll need ¼ cup of juice.

For the dressing: In a blender, blend the oil, vinegar, agave, and ¼ cup grapefruit juice until combined. Adjust proportions to taste.

Toss arugula and fennel with a little dressing at a time until coated. Add avocado and season with salt and pepper. Top with grapefruit segments and serve.

CHLOE'S TIP: FENNEL

Fennel is a root vegetable. Trim off the root and discard the green tops, as they are not edible. Take the bulb and cut it into quarters, then cut the inner core out of each quarter and discard. With a vegetable peeler, peel very thin slices of each quarter. You do not want thick shavings as they will be tough and hard to chew.

CHLOE'S TIP: HOW TO SEGMENT A GRAPEFRUIT

When you segment citrus fruits, you are making nice clean segments of the fruit so that it does not have the white membrane attached. To segment a grapefruit, begin by using a very sharp knife and trimming off the top and the bottom of the grapefruit. Then set the fruit cut side down on a cutting board and carefully cut the peel from the fruit. Start at the top and cut in ½ slices down to the base of the fruit. Then, hold the fruit in your hand and very carefully insert the knife between each segment and the membrane on both sides lifting each segment out. When you are finished, only the membrane will remain and you will have perfect wedges of grapefruit. You can squeeze remaining juice out of the membrane.

ROASTED CARROT AND AVOCADO SALAD*
INSALATA DI CAROTE ARROSTITE ED AVOCADO

SERVES 4

This recipe is inspired by one of my favorite spots in New York City, ABC Kitchen. It's a beautiful restaurant in the Flatiron District, featuring daily local produce from the Union Square Green Market on the menu. Back to the salad, I think the pairing of avocados and caramelized roasted carrots is pure genius, so after I tried something similar at ABC Kitchen, I naturally came home and whipped up my own version. My recipe tester Katie said the carrots remind her of french fries because they are so addicting!

MAKE-AHEAD TIP: Carrots can be roasted up to 3 days in advance and stored in the refrigerator.

RUSTIC CROUTONS

2 tablespoons olive oil

2 cups (1-inch) bread cubes

Sea salt

Freshly ground black pepper

8 carrots, peeled and ends trimmed

6 sprigs fresh thyme, plus extra for garnish

4 garlic cloves, unpeeled and left whole

Olive oil

Sea salt

Freshly ground black pepper

1 teaspoon Italian seasoning

¼ teaspoon ground cumin

2 cups baby arugula

Half a lemon

1 avocado, cubed

For the rustic croutons: In a large skillet, heat oil over medium heat and sauté bread cubes until lightly toasted, about 10 minutes. Adjust heat as needed. Season with salt and pepper while cooking. Set aside.

Preheat the oven to 400°F. On a large rimmed baking sheet, toss carrots, thyme, and garlic with enough olive oil to coat. Season with salt and pepper. Add Italian seasoning and cumin. Roast for 40 to 45 minutes until carrots are fork-tender and nicely browned, turning often with a spatula to prevent burning. Discard roasted thyme. The garlic can be peeled and spread on bread.

Place arugula in a large bowl and very lightly drizzle with oil. Squeeze with lemon juice, season with salt and pepper, and toss to coat. Season to taste.

For each serving, plate a portion of dressed arugula and top with two roasted carrots (warm or room temperature), avocado, and croutons. Garnish the salad with thyme leaves and serve.

ITALIAN CHOPPED SALAD
INSALATA SPEZZETTATA

SERVES 4

My brother Andy loves chopped salad like a vegan loves cupcakes. I remember him as a kid scarfing down large bowlfuls at every Italian restaurant we went to. He always asked for extra chickpeas (also known as garbanzo beans). I invented this salad with him in mind, complete with chickpeas, chopped tomatoes, kalamata olives, fresh basil, and tofu "mozzarella." I think my version tastes just as good as, if not better than, the original salami-and-cheese-laden salad. When my brother gave it two thumbs-up, I knew my work was done.

DRESSING

1 garlic clove, minced

1 tablespoon Dijon mustard

½ teaspoon sea salt

2 tablespoons red wine vinegar

½ cup olive oil

1 tablespoon agave

SALAD

1 head romaine, finely chopped

½ cup fresh basil, cut into a fine chiffonade, see Tip (page 26)

1 can chickpeas, rinsed and drained

1 tomato, chopped

½ cup kalamata olives, pitted and chopped

2 scallions, white and light green parts thinly sliced

7 ounces extra-firm tofu, drained and patted dry

Sea salt

Freshly ground black pepper

For the dressing: In a blender, combine all ingredients and blend until smooth. Store in refrigerator for up to 3 days.

For the salad: In a large bowl, toss romaine, basil, chickpeas, tomato, olives, and scallions. Finely crumble the tofu into the salad. Toss with desired amount of dressing and season with salt and pepper. Top each serving with more pepper.

SUMMER BREAD SALAD *
PANZANELLA

SERVES 6 TO 8 AS A STARTER; 4 AS A MEAL

If you're looking for a salad to impress, this is your ticket! There's nothing like a good Italian bread salad. The bread soaks up the flavors of the garlic and sweet balsamic, and the basil really seals the deal—it's kind of like eating tomato bruschetta with a fork. For a California twist, I've added avocado to the mix.

In a large skillet, heat 3 tablespoons of the oil over medium-high heat and add bread cubes. Season with salt, and let cook for 5 to 10 minutes, tossing frequently until lightly toasted.

In a large bowl, combine bread, cucumber, tomatoes, onion, and garlic. Drizzle with the remaining 1 tablespoon oil and the vinegar, and toss to coat. Season with salt and pepper, and let sit for 30 minutes at room temperature to allow flavors to blend. Toss in basil, arugula, and avocado right before serving.

4 tablespoons olive oil

3 cups (¾-inch) Italian bread cubes

Sea salt

1 cucumber, peeled, seeded, and chopped

3 large tomatoes, roughly chopped

½ small red onion, thinly sliced

1 garlic clove, minced

2 tablespoons balsamic vinegar

Freshly ground black pepper

2 cups fresh basil, torn into pieces

2 cups arugula

1 avocado, cubed

CREAM OF MUSHROOM SOUP
VELLUTATA DI FUNGHI

SERVES 4

Ditch the red can and whip up your own pot of homemade cream of mushroom soup! This soup may not be classically Italian, but I much prefer it to the more brothy Italian mushroom soups. I made this on a blustery New York night, and my roommate Esha took one taste, canceled her take-out food order, and nearly finished the entire pot with me. She couldn't believe there wasn't any cream!

MAKE-AHEAD TIP: Soup can be frozen for up to 1 month or refrigerated for up to 3 days. Reheat before serving.

2 tablespoons olive oil

1 onion, roughly chopped

1 pound white mushrooms, trimmed and coarsely chopped

1 garlic clove, minced

¼ cup dry white wine

3 cups water

2 teaspoons sea salt

½ cup canned coconut milk, mixed well before measuring

Freshly ground black pepper

¼ cup chopped fresh Italian parsley

In a large pot, heat oil over medium-high heat and cook onion and mushrooms until soft. Add garlic and cook for 1 minute more, until fragrant. Add wine and reduce until almost dry. Add water and salt, and whisk thoroughly. Bring to a boil, covered, then reduce heat and let simmer, covered, about 10 minutes.

In batches, transfer soup to a blender and puree until almost smooth. Return to the pot and stir in coconut milk. Reheat the soup. Season with pepper. Divide among bowls and garnish with parsley.

CAULIFLOWER SOUP WITH PESTO AND PASTA SHELLS
ZUPPA DI CAVOLFIORE CON CONCHIGLIONI AL PESTO GENOVESE

SERVES 4 TO 6

This soup can be served as an entrée. Succulent baby pasta shells swimming in thick and creamy cauliflower soup topped with a dollop of basil pesto makes for an oh-so-comforting supper.

NOTE: For a shortcut, purchase precut cauliflower florets at the grocery store.

MAKE-AHEAD TIP: Soup can be frozen for up to 1 month or refrigerated for up to 3 days. Reheat and top with pesto before serving.

Bring a large pot of salted water to a boil. Add shells and cook according to package directions. Drain and set aside.

In the large pot, heat oil over medium-high heat and add onion. Add 1 teaspoon of the salt and let cook until soft. Add garlic and let cook for 1 minute more, until fragrant. Add vegetable broth, cover, and bring to a boil. Add cauliflower and the remaining 1 teaspoon salt, cover again, and let simmer until cauliflower is fork-tender, 8 to 10 minutes.

In batches, transfer the soup to a blender and puree until smooth. Transfer back to the pot and stir in water, lemon juice, and cooked pasta shells. Season with pepper and distribute among serving bowls. Top each portion with a tablespoon of pesto sauce and swirl in. Serve immediately.

1 cup small brown rice pasta shells

2 tablespoons olive oil

1 onion, roughly chopped

2 teaspoons sea salt

3 garlic cloves, minced

2 cups vegetable broth

12 ounces cauliflower florets

1 cup water

2 teaspoons lemon juice

Freshly ground black pepper

Classic Pesto Sauce (page 233)

SPICY TOMATO SOUP*
ZUPPA DI POMODORO PICCANTE

SERVES 6

This ain't your average tomato soup! Don't expect a lot of conversation when serving this. Everyone will be busy eating this mildly spicy and wildly unique soup. Think sweet tomato soup with a touch of coconut milk, a kick of Italian spices, and oversized rustic croutons to break up the intense flavor. Omit the croutons to make it gluten-free!

MAKE-AHEAD TIP: Soup can be frozen for up to 1 month or refrigerated for up to 3 days. Reheat and top with coconut drizzle and croutons before serving.

SOUP

2 tablespoons olive oil

1 onion, roughly chopped

2 garlic cloves, minced

2 teaspoons sea salt

2 teaspoons Italian seasoning

¼ teaspoon crushed red pepper

1 (28-ounce) can fire-roasted whole tomatoes

3 cups vegetable broth

1 cup canned coconut milk, plus extra for drizzling

2 tablespoons brown sugar

Chopped fresh basil for garnish

RUSTIC CROUTONS

2 tablespoons olive oil

2 cups (1-inch) bread cubes

Sea salt

Freshly ground black pepper

For the soup: In a large pot, heat oil over medium-high heat and sauté onion until soft. Add garlic, salt, Italian seasoning, and red pepper, and let cook for 1 minute more, until fragrant. Add tomatoes and vegetable broth, and bring to a boil. Remove from heat, and in batches, transfer soup to a blender and puree until smooth. Return to the pot, stir in coconut milk and brown sugar, reheat, and season to taste.

For the croutons: In a large skillet, heat oil and sauté bread cubes until lightly toasted, about 10 minutes. Season with salt and pepper while cooking.

To serve: Distribute among bowls, top with a drizzle of coconut milk, basil, and croutons.

TORNARE CON L'EX E' COME MANGIARE UNA MINESTRA FREDDA.

(GOING BACK TO AN "EX" IS LIKE EATING COLD SOUP.)

PUMPKIN SOUP WITH CRISPY BRUSSELS SPROUT LEAVES
ZUPPA DI ZUCCA CON CROCCANTI FOGLIE DI CAVOLETTI DI BRUXELLES

SERVES 4

This soup uses canned pumpkin, which means you can make it year-round! If you have leftover Brussels sprout leaves, serve them in a dish on the table for snacking. Also, if you're making this soup for kids, leave out the cayenne or knock it down a little.

MAKE-AHEAD TIP: Soup can be frozen for up to 1 month or refrigerated for up to 3 days. Reheat and top with Brussels sprout leaves before serving.

For the soup: In a large pot, heat oil over medium-high heat and sauté onion and apple until soft, 10 to 15 minutes. Add garlic, salt, and cayenne, and let cook for 1 minute more, until fragrant. Add broth and pumpkin, and bring to a boil. Remove from heat, and in batches, transfer soup to a blender and puree until smooth. Return to the pot, stir in coconut milk and brown sugar, reheat, and season to taste.

For the crispy Brussels sprout leaves: Preheat the oven to 375°F.

Spread Brussels sprout leaves on a large rimmed baking sheet and toss with oil. Season with salt and pepper, and bake for 10 to 12 minutes until lightly browned and crisp.

To serve: Divide soup into bowls and top with a spoonful of crispy Brussels sprout leaves.

PUMPKIN SOUP

2 tablespoons olive oil

1 onion, roughly chopped

1 apple, unpeeled, cored, and sliced

1 garlic clove, minced

2 teaspoons sea salt

¼ teaspoon cayenne

3 cups vegetable broth

1 (15-ounce) can pumpkin puree

¾ cup canned coconut milk

2 tablespoons brown sugar

CRISPY BRUSSELS SPROUT LEAVES

4 ounces Brussels sprouts, trimmed and leaves separated

1 to 2 teaspoons olive oil

Sea salt

Freshly ground black pepper

TOMATO BREAD SOUP*

PAPPA AL POMODORO

SERVES 4 TO 6

This classic Italian soup is mind-blowingly delicious. My recipe tester Susan said she was shocked how flavorful it was from such simple ingredients. The bread cubes swell up like fat dumplings—think Italian matzo ball soup! In Italy they sometimes call it "bread gnocchi." The basil is your best friend in this dish, so don't leave it out.

¼ cup olive oil, plus extra for drizzling

1 large onion, finely chopped

3 garlic cloves, minced

¼ teaspoon crushed red pepper (optional)

2½ to 3 pounds very ripe tomatoes, cored and coarsely chopped

2 cups vegetable broth

2 teaspoons sea salt

¼ teaspoon freshly ground black pepper

3 cups day-old crusty bread, crusts removed, cut into 1-inch cubes

¼ cup fresh basil leaves, torn if large, plus extra for garnish

2 tablespoons brown sugar

1 tablespoon lemon juice

In a large pot, heat oil over medium-high heat. Add onion and cook, stirring often, until soft, about 10 minutes. Add garlic and red pepper, if using, and cook until fragrant, about 1 minute. Add tomatoes and cook, stirring often, until they begin to break down and release their liquid, about 5 minutes.

Add vegetable broth, salt, and pepper. Bring to a boil, then add bread and stir to combine. Reduce heat to low, cover, and simmer until bread is soft and soup thickens, about 15 minutes. Stir in basil, brown sugar, and lemon juice. Turn off heat and season to taste. Distribute into soup bowls, drizzle each serving with olive oil, and garnish with basil.

PIZZA, FOCACCIA, AND PANINI

(PIZZA, FOCÀCCIA, E PANINI)

This chapter is about all things doughy and bready. From traditional focaccia and pizza to more playful Italian-style sliders and bread sticks, these recipes all require eating with your hands and lots of napkins!

HEIRLOOM TOMATO TOAST*

TOAST CON POMODORI CUORE DI BUE

SERVES 3

Here are a few tips for turning this seemingly ordinary recipe into an out-of-this-world culinary creation. Pick juicy, ripe tomatoes. Get the bread nice and charred on the edges for crunch and smoky flavor. Be generous with the olive oil, salt, and pepper. The more you season, the brighter the flavor. That is all—enjoy!

6 slices multigrain bread

Olive oil

3 heirloom tomatoes, thinly sliced

Sea salt

Freshly ground black pepper

Preheat the oven to broil, set to high.

Place bread slices on a baking sheet and brush with oil. Broil for 1 to 2 minutes, checking frequently until lightly browned.

Fan tomato slices on toast and drizzle oil over the top. Season with salt and pepper. Serve immediately.

CHLOE'S TIP: CHOOSING INGREDIENTS

When a recipe has very few ingredients, each of them should be chosen with care. Not only should the tomatoes be at the peak of ripeness, but the bread should be the best quality. A local baker should be able to provide a vegan multigrain loaf or even an Italian-style roll that will make this recipe sing.

GARLIC BREAD STICKS

GRISSINI ALL'AGLIO

MAKES ABOUT 16 BREAD STICKS

DOUGH

¼ cup warm water
(about 110°F)

1 package active dry yeast
(2¼ teaspoons)

2 tablespoons sugar

1 cup soy, almond, or rice milk

3 tablespoons vegan margarine

1 teaspoon sea salt

4 cups all-purpose flour

Coarse salt for sprinkling

TOPPING

3 tablespoons vegan margarine

½ teaspoon garlic powder

½ teaspoon dried oregano

Sea salt

For the bread sticks: Line 2 large baking sheets with parchment paper.

Place warm water, yeast, and 1 tablespoon of the sugar in a 1-cup glass measuring cup. Stir for a second and set aside for about 10 minutes. The yeast will become foamy, double in size, and reach the ½-cup line. Meanwhile, heat the nondairy milk, margarine, salt, and the remaining 1 tablespoon sugar in a medium saucepan over medium heat until mixture is warm.

In the bowl of a mixer with a paddle or whisk attachment, combine the yeast mixture and the butter mixture. Beat for 1 minute. Add 2 cups of the flour and beat for 1 minute more. Add the remaining 2 cups flour and beat again for 1 minute. Transfer dough to a lightly floured surface and knead for 2 to 3 minutes until soft and pliable. Break off pieces of dough that are 2 to 3 inches long. Roll each piece between your hands until 7-inch ropes form, and place them on the pan. Repeat with all the dough.

Cover with a dry kitchen towel and place in a warm part of the kitchen. Let it sit until it has doubled in volume, about 45 minutes, see Tip (page 194).

For the topping: Combine all ingredients in a small saucepan and heat over medium heat until melted and spreadable.

Preheat the oven to 400°F. After the bread sticks have risen, uncover and bake for 8 to 10 minutes. Brush the hot bread sticks with the topping, repeat until all the topping is used. Sprinkle with coarse salt and serve while warm.

FABULOUS FOCACCIA

FOCÀCCIA AL ROSMARINO

MAKES ABOUT 24 (2-INCH) PIECES

The thought of homemade focaccia might make you shudder. Kneading? Rising? Rolling? No thanks! But truthfully, it's not so bad! This recipe is focaccia in its easiest and most foolproof form. Add whatever you'd like from the garden: tomatoes, eggplant, zucchini, and so on. I love the onion, olive, and rosemary combo. Making a "sponge" helps start the dough and activates the yeast.

SPONGE

1 tablespoon active dry yeast

1 teaspoon sugar

⅔ cup warm water (about 110°F)

½ cup all-purpose flour

DOUGH

1 small potato, peeled, cooked, and mashed (about 1 cup)

½ cup warm water

3 tablespoons olive oil, plus extra for brushing

1 tablespoon sea salt

1 teaspoon garlic powder

4 cups all-purpose flour, plus extra for work surface

Yellow cornmeal for sprinkling

Coarse salt for sprinkling

1 red onion, very thinly sliced

¾ cup kalamata olives, pitted

3 tablespoons fresh rosemary, chopped

For the sponge: Mix yeast, sugar, water, and flour in a large bowl (see Tip, page 194). Cover with a dry kitchen towel and place in a warm part of the kitchen. Let it rise for 30 minutes until foamy.

For the dough: Add potato, water, oil, salt, garlic powder, and flour to the sponge. Mix with a large spoon. If needed, add a little more water, 1 tablespoon at a time, until it comes together. Place the dough on a lightly floured surface and knead with your hands for about 10 minutes.

Transfer the dough to a large well-oiled bowl. Cover with a dry kitchen towel and place in a warm part of the kitchen. Let it sit until it has doubled in size, about 1½ hours.

Brush a large baking sheet with oil and sprinkle with cornmeal. After the dough has risen, punch it down, and stretch to form a large oval, about ½ inch thick, in the baking sheet. Cover with a dry kitchen towel and let it sit for 15 minutes.

Preheat the oven to 475°F.

Use your finger to create dimples in the dough and brush the top with oil. Sprinkle with coarse salt, onion, olives, and rosemary. Bake for 20 minutes or until lightly browned. Slice and serve while warm.

PIZZA MARGHERITA

PIZZA MARGHERITA

SERVES 4

This classic pizza is simple and delicious! Feel free to jazz it up with your favorite pizza toppings like sautéed mushrooms, onions, olives, or spinach.

NOTE: Use Gluten-Free Pizza Crust (page 235) if desired.

Olive oil for brushing and drizzling

1 tablespoon cornmeal

All-purpose flour for work surface

1 pound pizza dough

Garlic powder for seasoning

Sea salt

¾ cup tomato sauce

1 tomato, thinly sliced

Freshly ground black pepper

¼ cup Mozzarella Sauce (page 237)

Fresh basil leaves for topping

Crushed red pepper (optional)

Preheat the oven to 450°F. Lightly brush a large baking sheet (approximately 9 x 13 inches) with oil.

Sprinkle the the baking sheet with cornmeal. On a lightly floured surface, roll or stretch the dough into a large rectangle. Fit it into the baking sheet and brush with oil. Season with garlic powder and salt. Spread enough tomato sauce to cover the dough, leaving about a ¾-inch border. Top with tomato slices and drizzle with oil. Season with salt and pepper and bake for 15 to 20 minutes until edges are golden. Remove from oven, drizzle with mozzarella sauce, and arrange basil leaves, then bake for 1 minute. Remove from oven and let cool slightly before slicing. Season with red pepper, if using, before eating.

GARLIC AND ARTICHOKE PIZZA
PIZZA CON CARCIOFI ED AGLIO

SERVES 4

Preheat the oven to 450°F. Lightly brush a large baking sheet (approximately 9 x 13 inches) with oil.

Sprinkle the baking sheet with cornmeal. On a lightly floured surface, roll or stretch the dough into a large rectangle. Fit it into the baking sheet and brush with olive oil. Spread enough tomato sauce to cover the dough, leaving about a ¾-inch border. Top with tomato slices, artichokes, garlic, and capers. Season with salt and pepper and bake for 15 to 20 minutes until edges are golden. Remove from oven, drizzle with mozzarella sauce, then bake for 1 minute. Remove from oven and let cool slightly before slicing. If desired, season with red pepper before eating.

Olive oil for brushing and drizzling

1 tablespoon cornmeal

1 pound pizza dough

¾ cup tomato sauce

1 plum tomato, thinly sliced

1 cup artichoke hearts, drained and thinly sliced

2 garlic cloves, thinly sliced

1 to 2 tablespoons capers, drained

Sea salt

Freshly ground black pepper

¼ cup Mozzarella Sauce (page 237)

Crushed red pepper (optional)

BUTTERNUT SQUASH, CARAMELIZED ONION, AND APPLE PIZZA *

PIZZA CON ZUCCA, MELE E CIPOLLE CARAMELLATE

SERVES 4

Sweet roasted butternut squash, caramelized onions, and tart and juicy apple slices top a garlicky white bean puree. Anyone who misses the cheese on this has lost their marbles.

For the roasted squash: Preheat the oven to 400°F. Spread butternut squash on a large rimmed baking sheet and toss with oil. Season with salt and pepper and roast for 30 to 35 minutes, until very tender when pierced with a fork. Remove from oven and set aside.

For the topping: In a large skillet, heat 2 tablespoons oil over medium-high heat and sauté onion until soft and lightly caramelized, about 20 minutes. Adjust heat as needed. Season with salt and pepper. Add apple and let cook 5 to 7 minutes until soft, adding more oil as needed. Add spinach and let cook until wilted.

For the garlic white bean puree: Combine beans, oil, lemon juice, garlic, thyme, salt, and pepper in a food processor, and process until completely smooth. Add water as needed.

Preheat the oven to 450°F. Lightly brush a large baking sheet (approximately 9 x 13 inches) with oil.

Sprinkle the baking sheet with cornmeal. On a lightly floured surface, roll or stretch the dough into a large rectangle. Fit it into the baking sheet and brush with oil.

Spread a thin layer of the puree evenly over the dough and arrange the squash and toppings. Season with salt and pepper, and drizzle with oil.

Bake for 15 to 20 minutes, rotating midway, until edges are golden. Let cool slightly before slicing.

ROASTED SQUASH

2 cups (½-inch) cubes peeled butternut squash

2 tablespoons olive oil

Sea salt

Freshly ground black pepper

TOPPING

2 tablespoons olive oil

1 onion, thinly sliced

Sea salt

Freshly ground black pepper

1 apple, peeled and thinly sliced

5 ounces baby spinach

GARLIC WHITE BEAN PUREE

1 (15-ounce) can cannellini or other white beans, rinsed and drained

¼ cup olive oil, plus extra for brushing and drizzling

1 tablespoon lemon juice

2 garlic cloves

½ teaspoon dried thyme

1 teaspoon sea salt

½ teaspoon freshly ground black pepper

1 to 2 tablespoons water

1 tablespoon cornmeal

1 pound pizza dough

FRENCH BREAD PIZZA*
PIZZA CON IMPASTO ALLA FRANCESE

SERVES 4

You don't always need a brick oven to bake up crusty pizzas. For this recipe, a loaf of French bread is the perfect easy way to make weeknight pizza. I absolutely love how the edges of the bread get so crisp. Feel free to swap the tomato sauce for Classic Pesto Sauce (page 233) and use whatever ingredients you have on hand for the toppings.

CARAMELIZED ONIONS

2 tablespoons olive oil

1 onion, thinly sliced

Sea salt

Freshly ground black pepper

1 tablespoon olive oil, plus extra for brushing

8 ounces mushrooms, trimmed and very thinly sliced

5 ounces baby spinach

4 mini sandwich rolls, halved (or about eight 4-inch pieces cut from a large loaf)

1 cup tomato sauce

1 cup kalamata olives, pitted and chopped

Crushed red pepper (optional for topping)

For the caramelized onions: In a large skillet, heat 2 tablespoons oil over medium heat and sauté onion until soft and lightly caramelized, 20 to 30 minutes. Adjust heat as needed. Season with salt and pepper. Transfer to a bowl, reserve skillet, and set aside.

To assemble the pizza: In the reserved skillet add 1 tablespoon of the olive oil and heat over medium-high heat. Add mushrooms and let cook until soft and most of the mushroom liquid has evaporated. Season with salt and pepper. Add spinach and let cook until spinach is wilted.

Preheat the oven to 450°F. Brush each piece of bread with oil on all sides and place on a large baking sheet, cut side up.

Spread enough tomato sauce to cover the bread. Top with caramelized onions, mushrooms, spinach, and olives. Season with salt and pepper, and bake for about 7 minutes, until edges are nicely browned. If desired, season with red pepper before eating.

CRUMBLED SAUSAGE AND MOZZARELLA PIZZA
PIZZA CON SALSICCIA SBRICIOLATA E MOZZARELLA

SERVES 4

Sweet mother of sausage! This pizza is the ultimate vegan paradise. The homemade sausage is so succulent that you could even leave out the Mozzarella Sauce for a quick fix.

MAKE-AHEAD TIP: Sausage can be made up to 3 days in advance and stored in the refrigerator. Assemble and bake entire pizza before serving.

SAUSAGE

1 cup walnuts

8 ounces sliced mushrooms

3 tablespoons all-purpose flour

1 teaspoon dried basil

1 teaspoon dried fennel

Pinch of crushed red pepper

1 teaspoon sea salt

1 teaspoon ground black pepper

1 tablespoon maple syrup

2 tablespoons olive oil, plus extra for brushing

1 tablespoon cornmeal

All-purpose flour for work surface

1 pound pizza dough

1 cup tomato sauce

Optional toppings: caramelized onions, fresh basil, sliced tomato

¾ cup Mozzarella Sauce (page 237)

Crushed red pepper (optional)

For the sausage: Place walnuts in a food processor, and process until a fine crumbly meal forms. Add mushrooms, flour, basil, fennel, red pepper, salt, pepper, and maple syrup, and pulse for about 25 times, until mushrooms are finely chopped. Do not overprocess; it should be somewhat crumbly and chunky.

Heat oil in a large nonstick skillet over medium-high heat. Transfer mushroom mixture to the pan and let cook, turning frequently with a spatula, and breaking up into medium-sized clumps until the mixture is evenly browned and crisp (about 15 minutes). Adjust heat as needed and add more oil if needed. Set aside.

Preheat the oven to 450°F. Lightly brush a large baking sheet (approximately 9 x 13 inches) with oil.

Sprinkle the baking sheet with cornmeal. On a lightly floured surface, roll or stretch the dough into a large rectangle. Fit it into the baking sheet and brush with oil. Spread enough tomato sauce over the dough, leaving about a ¾-inch border. Top with crumbled sausage and any optional toppings. Bake for 15 to 20 minutes until edges are golden. Remove from oven, drizzle with mozzarella sauce, then bake for 1 minute. Remove from oven and let cool slightly before slicing. If desired, season with red pepper before eating.

WHITE WILD MUSHROOM PIZZA *
PIZZA BIANCA CON FUNGHI SELVATICI

SERVES 4

I hosted a taste-testing party in New York City for some old college friends to test this pizza. I made the mistake of having it during an "important" football game, and one of the guys actually took out his laptop and turned on the game during dinner. Nobody paid attention to the food until one of them took a bite of this pizza. "Phenomenal" and "life-changing" were a couple of the adjectives used. This pizza is the ultimate touchdown!

2 tablespoons olive oil, plus extra for brushing

8 ounces white mushrooms, trimmed and sliced

3 large shallots, sliced

½ teaspoon sea salt

¼ teaspoon freshly ground black pepper

¼ cup white wine

1 teaspoon fresh thyme leaves, plus extra for garnish

1 tablespoon chopped fresh Italian parsley

8 ounces wild or mixed mushrooms, trimmed and sliced

1 tablespoon cornmeal

1 pound pizza dough

2 garlic cloves, minced

¼ cup Mozzarella Sauce (page 237)

Chili olive oil (store-bought or recipe on page 238) for drizzling

In a medium skillet, heat 1 tablespoon of the oil over medium-high heat and sauté mushrooms, shallots, salt, and pepper, until mushrooms and shallots are soft and lightly browned. Add wine, reduce heat to medium-low, and let cook until most of the liquid evaporates. Turn off the heat, and mix in thyme and parsley. Season to taste and let cool slightly. Transfer mushroom mixture to a food processor and reserve the skillet. Pulse a few times until mushrooms are finely chopped into a spread-like consistency.

In the reserved skillet, heat the remaining tablespoon oil over medium-high heat and sauté wild mushrooms until very soft. Season with salt and pepper, and set aside.

Preheat the oven to 450°F. Lightly brush a large baking sheet (approximately 9 x 13 inches) with oil.

Sprinkle the baking sheet with cornmeal. On a lightly floured surface, roll or stretch the dough into a large rectangle. Fit it into the baking sheet and brush with oil. Sprinkle with garlic, leaving a ¾-inch border. Spread the pulsed mushroom mixture and arrange the sautéed wild mushrooms on top. Season with salt and pepper and bake for 15 to 20 minutes, until edges are golden. Remove from oven, drizzle with mozzarella sauce, then bake for 1 minute. Remove from oven and let cool slightly before slicing. Drizzle with chili oil and garnish with thyme.

GRILLED PESTO PIE
TORTA SALATA AL PESTO GENOVESE

SERVES 6

Have you ever seen a bear eat after hibernation? Me neither, but I imagine it looks something like when my brother dug into this Grilled Pesto Pie! He demanded seconds, thirds, fourths, and all he could murmur was "keep 'em coming!" as he nearly swallowed them whole. Who could blame him? They are delicious.

Preheat a grill or stovetop grill pan to medium-high heat.

Cut pizza dough into 6 equal pieces. On a lightly floured surface, roll each piece of dough into a 6-inch circle. The circle should be as thin as a tortilla. Lightly brush both sides of the dough with oil and grill for 3 to 5 minutes on one side, until the bottom is lightly browned. If needed, adjust the heat of the grill. Using tongs, flip the dough and immediately spread pesto on the already-browned side. Top with ricotta and sun-dried tomatoes. Let cook on grill for another 3 to 5 minutes and remove from heat. Repeat this process with the remaining dough.

1 to 1½ pounds pizza dough

Olive oil for brushing

Classic Pesto Sauce (page 233)

Rockin' Ricotta (page 242)

½ cup sun-dried tomatoes, finely chopped

PUPPY PIZZA BONES

MAKES ABOUT 50 BONES FOR YOUR FOUR-LEGGED FRIEND

Preheat the oven to 350°F.

In a large bowl mix all ingredients with a large spoon or your hands. Form the dough into 1½-inch disks or bones and bake on a large baking sheet for 30 minutes. Let cool completely and cut into pieces if necessary according to your dog's size.

2 cups whole wheat flour

1 tablespoon olive oil

¾ cup water

1½ teaspoons baking powder

½ cup finely chopped spinach

½ cup finely chopped carrots

MEATBALL SLIDERS*
PANINETTI CON POLPETTE

MAKES ABOUT 20 MEATBALLS

I made these once for a pack of far-from-vegan guy friends and they scarfed them down. They were shocked to learn that they were vegetarian, let alone vegan! Trust me—this is your new dinner party go-to recipe.

MAKE-AHEAD TIP: The meatball mixture can be made in advance, shaped into balls, and kept refrigerated or frozen until ready to panfry. Pesto Sauce can be made in advance and kept refrigerated for up to 5 days.

MEATBALLS

2 tablespoons olive oil, plus extra for brushing

1 onion, finely chopped

8 ounces sliced mushrooms

2 garlic cloves, minced

1½ cups cooked brown rice, cooled

½ cup Italian bread crumbs

¼ cup all-purpose flour

1 teaspoon dried basil

1½ teaspoons sea salt

1 teaspoon freshly ground black pepper

¼ teaspoon crushed red pepper (optional)

Canola oil for frying

Slider buns or dinner rolls

1 cup tomato sauce, heated

Classic Pesto Sauce (page 233)

Fresh basil leaves for assembly

For the meatballs: Heat olive oil in a large nonstick skillet over medium-high heat, and cook onion and mushrooms until soft and lightly browned. Add garlic and cook a few more minutes. Transfer to a food processor. Reserve skillet for later use.

Add cooled brown rice, bread crumbs, flour, basil, salt, pepper, and red pepper, if using, to the food processor. Pulse until the mixture just comes together. If necessary, transfer the mixture to a large bowl and mix with your hands. Season to taste and let cool slightly. Form the mixture into 1- or 2-inch balls to fit your bun size.

Heat canola oil in the reserved nonstick skillet over medium-high heat, and panfry meatballs in batches, adding more oil as needed.

Slice slider buns in half and brush the insides with olive oil. Toast in a sauté pan over medium heat until lightly browned on the edges. Layer a spoonful of tomato sauce, a meatball, a spoonful of pesto sauce, and a basil leaf in each slider bun. Stick each slider with a party pick to hold it together. Serve immediately.

MUSHROOM PESTO SLIDERS *
PANINETTI CON PESTO DI FUNGHI

MAKES ABOUT 16 SLIDERS

These sliders are really easy to make and "taste just like meat!" according to my roommates. I make these often for business lunches because they're super flavorful and everyone always loves them. A small batch of my quick basil pesto is the perfect topping and speeds up the process.

MAKE-AHEAD TIP: Uncooked slider patties can be formed in advance and kept refrigerated or frozen until ready to panfry. Caramelized onions can also be made the day before serving and stored in the refrigerator.

For the caramelized onions: In a large skillet, heat oil and sauté onion over medium heat until tender and slightly caramelized, 20 to 30 minutes. Season with salt and pepper and set aside.

For the sliders: In a large nonstick skillet, heat oil over medium-high heat and sauté mushrooms until just soft. Remove from heat and let cool a few minutes. Transfer mushrooms to a food processor and set skillet aside for later use.

Add lentils, flour, basil, salt, and pepper to the processor. Pulse until the mixture just comes together. Refrigerate the mixture until chilled. If the mixture is too sticky, you can add a little bit more flour. Using the palms of your hands, form the mixture into mini patties, each about 2 inches in diameter by ½ inch thick.

Heat the reserved skillet over medium-high heat, and fry patties in batches, adding more oil as needed. Let the patties cook 3 to 5 minutes on each side, or until nicely browned.

Assemble sliders by layering the slider patty, basil pesto, caramelized onions, and tomato on the buns.

CARAMELIZED ONIONS

2 tablespoons olive oil

1 large red onion, thinly sliced

Sea salt

Freshly ground black pepper

SLIDERS

1 tablespoon olive oil, plus extra for frying

8 ounces mushrooms, sliced

1 (15-ounce) can lentils, rinsed and drained (or 2 cups cooked)

¾ cup all-purpose flour, plus extra if needed

1 teaspoon dried basil

1 teaspoon sea salt

1 teaspoon freshly ground black pepper

Quick Basil Pesto (page 232)

Mini buns or dinner rolls, sliced in half and toasted

1 small tomato, thinly sliced

FARMERS' MARKET PANINI
PANINO CON LE VERDURE LOCALI

SERVES 4

Tangy balsamic grilled eggplant, fresh basil, sweet and juicy tomatoes, creamy avocado, and savory garlic white bean puree are layered into a hot and crusty panini. The eggplant and bean puree can be prepared in advance, which makes the assembly that much easier.

BALSAMIC GRILLED EGGPLANT

1 small eggplant, very thinly sliced lengthwise

Sea salt

Olive oil for brushing

Balsamic vinegar for drizzling

WHITE BEAN SPREAD

1 (15-ounce) can white beans, rinsed and drained

¼ cup olive oil

1 tablespoon water

1 tablespoon lemon juice

1 garlic clove

¾ teaspoon sea salt

½ teaspoon freshly ground black pepper

8 slices of bread

1 heirloom or regular tomato, sliced

½ red onion, sliced

½ cup fresh basil

1 avocado, sliced

Sea salt

Freshly ground black pepper

For the balsamic grilled eggplant: Lay the eggplant slices on a tray and salt one side liberally. This will "sweat" the eggplant and get rid of any bitter taste. After about 20 minutes, wipe the salt and released moisture from the eggplant with a paper towel, or rinse in a colander and pat dry.

Preheat a grill or grill pan to medium-high.

Brush both sides of the eggplant slices with oil. Grill on both sides until each slice becomes tender with prominent grill marks. I use tongs while flipping for best control. Remove from heat and drizzle with vinegar.

For the white bean spread: Combine beans, oil, water, lemon juice, garlic, salt, and pepper in a food processor and process until smooth. Add salt to taste. Set aside.

To assemble the panini: Preheat a panini press to high. If you don't have one, heat a lightly oiled skillet or griddle.

Brush both sides of each bread slice with oil. Then, drizzle the insides of each slice with vinegar and season with salt and pepper. For each panino, spread both slices with the white bean spread. Layer 2 slices of eggplant, tomato, onion, basil, and avocado, and season with salt and pepper. Brush the top and bottom of each panino with oil. Press on a hot panini press until nice grill marks appear. Slice panini in half diagonally and serve immediately.

CHICKPEA PIE
FARINATA DI CÉCI

SERVES 8

You may have heard of the newly famous chickpea pie by one of its million names: farinata, torta di céci, socca, karantita, and the list goes on. Many cultures have a variation of this gluten-free breadlike pie made from chickpea (same as garbanzo) flour and flavored with whatever your heart desires. This is the basic recipe, but feel free to get creative with add-ins: fresh herbs, thinly sliced onions, chopped tomatoes, sautéed mushrooms, and so on.

NOTE: The batter will need to sit for at least 2 hours before baking.

In a medium bowl, mix water and flour until combined. Cover with plastic wrap and let sit for at least 2 hours.

After 2 hours, preheat the oven to 500°F. Place a 9- or 10-inch cast-iron skillet in the heated oven and let heat for 10 minutes.

Meanwhile, skim the foam off the flour mixture. Stir in 3 tablespoons of the oil, salt, and rosemary. Carefully remove the hot-cast iron skillet and add a splash of oil to swirl around and grease the skillet. Carefully pour the batter into the skillet and bake for 22 to 25 minutes until lightly browned and crisp. Run a knife around the edges and unmold onto a cutting board. Season with salt and pepper, if needed. Slice like a pizza and serve warm.

2 cups warm water

1½ cups garbanzo flour
(or garbanzo and fava flour)

3 tablespoons olive oil, plus
more for pan

1 teaspoon sea salt

1 teaspoon chopped fresh
rosemary

Freshly ground black pepper

RED WINE SEITAN ON CIABATTA*
SEITAN AL VINO ROSSO SU PANE CIABATTA

SERVES 4

Okay, okay, so I keep saying that every recipe is the best recipe in the world, but trust me, this one really is! Grilled seitan slathered in sticky red wine barbecue sauce on toasted ciabatta with caramelized onions—handheld heaven!

MAKE-AHEAD TIP: *Barbecue seitan and caramelized onions can be made the day before and stored separately in the refrigerator.*

CARAMELIZED ONIONS

2 tablespoons olive oil

1 large onion, thinly sliced

Sea salt

2 teaspoons maple syrup

BARBECUE SEITAN

1 cup ketchup

¼ cup dry red wine

1 tablespoon balsamic vinegar, plus extra for drizzling

1 tablespoon brown sugar

1 teaspoon Dijon mustard

1 teaspoon onion powder

½ teaspoon freshly ground black pepper

2 tablespoons olive oil, plus extra for brushing

1 large shallot, thinly sliced (about ½ cup)

8 ounces seitan, cut into thin strips

3 scallions, trimmed and thinly sliced

4 ciabatta rolls

1 cup arugula

1 small tomato, thinly sliced

For the caramelized onions: In a large skillet, heat oil over medium heat and add onion. Season with salt and let cook, stirring frequently, until very soft, about 20 minutes. Add maple syrup and let cook for 1 minute more. Remove from heat and set aside.

For the barbecue seitan: In a small bowl, make sauce by whisking ketchup, wine, vinegar, brown sugar, mustard, onion powder, and pepper. Set aside.

In a large skillet, heat oil over medium-high heat and cook shallot and seitan until lightly browned.

Add sauce and scallions to skillet. Reduce heat to low, and let simmer until sauce has thickened, about 5 minutes.

Slice the rolls in half, brush the insides with oil, and drizzle with vinegar. Toast in a sauté pan over medium heat until lightly browned on the edges. Layer a small handful of arugula, seitan, tomato, and caramelized onions on each roll and serve.

PIZZA BURGERS WITH AVOCADO PESTO

HAMBURGER DI PIZZA CON PESTO DI AVOCADO

SERVES 6

California meets Italy in these tangy pizza burgers layered with creamy avocado pesto.

MAKE-AHEAD TIP: Uncooked patties can be formed in advance and kept refrigerated or frozen until ready to panfry.

AVOCADO PESTO

1 avocado

1 garlic clove

½ cup packed fresh basil

1 tablespoon lemon juice

½ teaspoon sea salt

¼ teaspoon freshly ground black pepper

¼ cup water

PATTIES

1 (15-ounce) can white beans, rinsed and drained

1 garlic clove

¾ cup chopped sun-dried tomatoes

½ cup packed fresh basil, plus extra for assembly

¼ cup bread crumbs

¼ cup all-purpose flour

1 teaspoon sea salt

¼ teaspoon freshly ground black pepper

2 tablespoons olive oil

Hamburger buns, lightly toasted

Optional toppings: sliced red onion, sliced tomato, fresh basil, ketchup

For the avocado pesto: Combine all ingredients in a food processor and process until smooth.

For the patties: Place beans, garlic, sun-dried tomatoes, basil, bread crumbs, flour, salt, and pepper in a food processor and pulse until just combined, stopping frequently to scrape down sides. Using the palms of your hands, form mixture into 6 or 7 (3-inch) patties.

In a large nonstick skillet, heat oil over medium-high heat and panfry patties, letting them cook for 3 to 5 minutes on each side. Once patties are nicely browned, remove from heat and drain on paper towels.

To serve: For each burger, layer a patty, a dollop of avocado pesto, and any desired additional toppings on the bun. Serve immediately.

AVOCADO AND SUN-DRIED TOMATO PANINI*

PANINO CON POMODORO SECCO DE AVOCADO

SERVES 4

Mmm, avocado layered with sweet sun-dried tomatoes grilled into a crispy panino brushed with olive oil and balsamic vinegar. So simple and divine.

4 ciabatta rolls, halved,
or 8 slices sandwich bread

Balsamic vinegar for drizzling

Sea salt

Freshly ground black pepper

½ cup baby spinach

½ red onion, very thinly sliced

1 avocado, thinly sliced

Olive oil for brushing

½ cup chopped sun-dried
tomatoes

Preheat a panini press to high. If you don't have a panini press, heat a lightly oiled skillet or griddle.

Drizzle the inside of each bread slice with vinegar and season with salt and pepper. Layer spinach, onion, and avocado on each bottom bread slice. Season the avocado with salt and pepper. Top the avocado with sun-dried tomatoes and then add the top bread slice. Brush the top and bottom of each panino with oil. Press on a hot panini press until nice grill marks appear. Slice panini in half diagonally and serve immediately.

VIVA LA PASTA

Regular dried white pasta that you buy at the grocery store is always vegan (though it doesn't hurt to check the ingredients). Fresh pasta that you might order at a restaurant, however, usually contains eggs. When I order pasta at non-vegan restaurants, I always request dried pasta to make sure it's vegan. For a quick weeknight dinner, dried pasta can be used for all of my pasta recipes. It's your choice whether to use white or whole wheat pasta, or gluten-free brown rice or quinoa noodles. I generally prefer white pasta or brown rice pasta due to the soft bite they lend, although occasionally I note otherwise for certain dishes. And of course, if you want to make your own fresh vegan pasta, try the recipe on page 236.

USE YOUR NOODLE!

Different pasta shapes work better with different kinds of sauces. Choose the pasta shape that most resembles the shape of the other ingredients in the sauce. If your sauce has ingredients that have been cut in long strips such as sliced bell peppers or mushrooms, they go better with longer shapes of pasta such as spaghetti or fettuccine. Scooped or dome-shaped pastas such as conchiglie or orecchiette will "catch" small ingredients such as peas or diced vegetables. Thin strands of pasta such as capellini or vermicelli pair well with thin oil-based sauces, while thicker pastas such as spaghetti or bucatini do well with thick chunky sauces.

Farfalle (far-FAH-leh): **bowties or butterflies**

Penne (PEN-neh): **"pens" or smooth cylinders**

Penne Rigate (PEN-neh re-GA-tay): **penne that has ridges**

Conchiglie (con-KEEL-yay): **seashells**

Gnocchi (NYO-kee): **small potato dumplings**

Fusilli (foo-ZEE-lee): **corkscrew pasta**

Rotelle (row-TELL-e): **wagon wheels**

Orecchiette (oh-reck-ee-ET-tay): **"little ears"**

Bucatini (boo-cah-TEE-nee): **long strands with a hole through the center (from "buco," which means hole)**

Spaccatelli (spah-cah-TELL-lee): **long strand with a slit down the entire strand**

Manicotti (mah-nih-CUT-tee): **"sleeves" larger than penne and stuffed**

Lasagna (la-ZAHN-yeh): **very wide noodles used for layering**

Radiatore (rah-dee-ah-TOR-eh): **"small radiators" or short and ruffled noodles**

Linguine (ling-gwee-nee): **thin flat noodles**

Fettuccine (feh-too-CHEE-nay): **long and flat strands that are wider than linguine**

Rotini (ro-teen-neh): **corkscrew pasta with a tighter helix than fusilli**

Capellini (cah-peh-LEE-nee): **long, very fine, strands or "angel hair"**

Spaghetti (spah-GET-tee): **long rounded noodles**

Orzo (OR-zoh): **means "barley," shaped like a grain of rice**

Ditalini (dee-tah-LEE-nee): **"little thimbles" or very short tubes used in soups or cold pasta salads**

Gemelli (jeh-MEL-iee): **means "twins" for two twisted strands of pasta**

Last thing, noodle lovers: Do not rinse your pasta after draining, or add oil. A little starch from the cooking water will help the pasta absorb the sauce. Adding oil will prevent the sauce from clinging to the pasta.

CAPELLINI POMODORO
CAPELLINI AL POMODORO

SERVES 4 TO 6

This simple pasta can be served as a main or side dish, and it can also be eaten cold the next day. The delicate capellini noodles pair perfectly with the light olive oil sauce, allowing the tomatoes, garlic, and fresh basil to really shine.

Bring a large pot of salted water to a boil. Add capellini and cook according to package directions. Drain and return to the pot. Toss noodles with 1 tablespoon of the oil and set aside.

Meanwhile, heat the remaining tablespoon oil in a medium skillet over medium-high heat. Add tomatoes and let cook until soft, about 15 minutes. Add garlic and salt and let cook a few more minutes. Remove from heat.

Add tomatoes and basil to pasta. Toss and season with pepper. Drizzle more oil as needed.

1 pound capellini
(or gluten-free pasta)

2 tablespoons olive oil,
plus more as needed

1 pound cherry tomatoes,
halved

2 garlic cloves, minced

2 teaspoons sea salt

1 cup fresh basil, cut into
chiffonade, see Tip (page 26)

Freshly ground black pepper

MAMA'S SPAGHETTI AND MEATBALLS
SPAGHETTI CON LE POLPETTINE

SERVES 4 TO 6

You can take a shortcut with a jar of marinara sauce. Throw some frozen broccoli florets into the boiling pasta water for the remaining five minutes for extra heartiness. The meatball mixture can be made in advance, shaped into balls, and kept refrigerated for up to 5 days.

MEATBALLS

2 tablespoons olive oil

1 onion, finely chopped

8 ounces cremini mushrooms, trimmed and sliced

2 garlic cloves, minced

1½ cups cooked brown rice, cooled

½ cup Italian bread crumbs

¼ cup all-purpose flour

1 teaspoon dried basil

1½ teaspoons sea salt

1 teaspoon freshly ground black pepper

¼ teaspoon crushed red pepper (optional)

Canola oil for frying

PASTA

1 pound spaghetti

1 (26-ounce) jar marinara sauce (or see recipe, page 234)

¼ cup soy, almond, or rice milk

2 tablespoons brown sugar

Sea salt

Freshly ground black pepper

¼ cup chopped fresh Italian parsley for garnish

Parmesan Topping (page 244)

For the meatballs: Heat olive oil in a large nonstick skillet over medium-high heat, and cook onion and mushrooms until soft and lightly browned. Add garlic and cook a few more minutes. Transfer to a food processor. Reserve the skillet for later use.

Add cooled brown rice, bread crumbs, flour, basil, salt, pepper, and red pepper, if using, to the food processor. Pulse until the mixture just comes together. If necessary, transfer the mixture to a large bowl and mix with your hands. Season to taste and let cool slightly. Form the mixture into 1- to 2-inch balls.

Heat canola oil in the reserved nonstick skillet over medium-high heat, and panfry meatballs in batches, adding more oil as needed. Rotate the meatballs with a wooden spoon so they are very well done. They should be browned on all sides with a nice crust. Remove meatballs from the pan using a slotted spoon and drain on paper towels.

For the pasta: Bring a large pot of salted water to a boil. Add spaghetti and cook according to package directions. Drain and return to the pot.

For the sauce: Combine marinara sauce, nondairy milk, and brown sugar in a medium pot. Stir over medium heat until heated through. Season with salt and pepper.

Add sauce to pasta and toss to coat. Top with meatballs, and garnish with parsley and Parmesan topping.

KATE MIDDLETON'S PASTA ALFREDO*
CAVOLFIORE ALL'ALFREDO ALLA KATE MIDDLETON

SERVE 4 TO 6

I named this after Kate Middleton because I always fantasize about what I would cook for her if she came over for lunch. Well, it would surely be this decadent pasta Alfredo because it is absolutely perfect, just like her! She would ask about the secret ingredient, and I would tell her it is pureed cauliflower—healthy, delicious, gluten-free, and fit for royalty. She'd jot down the recipe and go home and cook it for Prince William!

For a shortcut, purchase precut cauliflower at the grocery store.

NOTE: If sauce thickens too much as it sits, reconstitute the pasta by adding a little bit of water or nondairy milk. Stir over medium heat until smooth. Adjust seasoning again to taste.

12 ounces cauliflower florets, not frozen

5 garlic cloves, peeled and left whole

1 onion, sliced

¼ cup olive oil

1½ teaspoons sea salt

1 pound brown rice penne or fusilli

2 cups almond milk

2 tablespoons lemon juice

Freshly ground black pepper

Chopped fresh Italian parsley for garnish

Parmesan Topping (page 244)

Preheat the oven to 425°F.

Spread cauliflower, garlic, and onion on a large rimmed baking sheet and drizzle with oil. Season with 1 teaspoon of the salt, then roast for about 30 minutes, or until cauliflower is fork-tender, turning frequently with a spatula. Add more oil as needed.

Meanwhile, bring a large pot of salted water to a boil. Add pasta and cook according to package directions. Drain and return to the pot.

Transfer roasted vegetables to a blender and add almond milk, lemon juice, and the remaining ½ teaspoon salt. Blend until very smooth. Adjust seasoning to taste, remove from blender, and toss with hot pasta. Season with pepper, and top with parsley and Parmesan topping. Serve immediately.

SHELLEY'S SHELLS
CONCHIGLIE ALLA SHELLEY

SERVES 4 TO 6

This is my mom Shelley's famous recipe for green pepper and onion shells, the best pasta in the world. Okay, I know it may sound rather plain, but it's anything but that! Once you cook down the onions and peppers, they become soft and caramelized with a creamy texture, and then tossed with hot shells and sea salt . . . I'm drooling just writing about it! This recipe goes back generations, so if it ain't broke, don't fix it!

NOTE: For a shortcut, use precut onions to save yourself some tears.

4 tablespoons olive oil

3 large green bell peppers, finely chopped

3 large onions, finely chopped

2 teaspoons sea salt

1 pound medium shells (or gluten-free pasta)

Freshly ground black pepper

In a large skillet, heat 2 tablespoons of the oil over medium-high heat and add bell peppers and onions. Add 1 teaspoon of the salt, and cook until very soft and lightly browned, about 20 minutes. If needed, add a little oil or water to pan to keep vegetables from sticking.

Meanwhile, bring a large pot of salted water to a boil. Add shells and cook according to package directions. Drain and return to the pot.

Toss pasta with the remaining 2 tablespoons oil, the remaining 1 teaspoon salt, and bell pepper and onion mixture. Season with pepper and adjust salt to taste.

CAVATELLI WITH BROCCOLI
CAVATELLI CON BROCCOLI

SERVES 4 TO 6

My recipe tester Ann Marie loved this dish because it's ready in ten minutes and it's healthy. So simple and perfect for a family of picky broccoli eaters. Delish!

Bring a large pot of salted water to a boil. Add cavatelli and cook according to package directions. Add broccoli for the last 5 minutes of boiling and let cook until broccoli is fork-tender. Reserve ½ cup of cooking water, then drain pasta and broccoli, and return to the pot.

Meanwhile, in a small skillet, heat oil over medium-high heat and add garlic. Cook for 1 minute until fragrant, then remove from heat and add to the pot of pasta. Add reserved pasta water and salt to the pasta, and toss to coat. Season with black pepper and red pepper, if using, to taste.

1 pound cavatelli
(or gluten-free pasta)

1 pound broccoli florets,
fresh or frozen

¼ cup olive oil

4 garlic cloves, minced

1 teaspoon sea salt

Freshly ground black pepper

Crushed red pepper (optional)

A TAVOLA NON SI INVECCHIA MAI.
(NOBODY EVER AGES AT THE DINNER TABLE.)

BOWTIES IN GARLIC CREAM SAUCE
FARFALLE ALLA CREMA DI AGLIO

SERVES 4 TO 6

This is one of my favorite pastas in the world—creamy farfalle pasta with sun-dried tomatoes and mushrooms. I've hosted millions (well, maybe not millions) of dinner parties and served this pasta, and no one ever thinks it's vegan. May it bring you the same dinner-party fortune!

NOTE: If sauce thickens too much as it sits, reconstitute the pasta by adding a little water or non-dairy milk. Stir over medium heat until smooth. Adjust seasoning again to taste.

Bring a large pot of salted water to a boil. Add farfalle and cook according to package directions. Right before draining, add sun-dried tomatoes to the boiling water. Then drain and return to the pot.

Meanwhile, heat 1 tablespoon of the oil in a medium skillet over medium-high heat. Add onion and let cook until soft. Add garlic and cook for 1 minute more. Remove from heat. In a blender, combine onion, cashews, water, lemon juice, and salt. Process on high until very smooth, about 2 minutes. Set aside.

In a large pot or skillet, heat the remaining 1 tablespoon olive oil over medium-high heat. Add mushrooms, season with salt and pepper, and cook until soft and lightly browned. If needed, add more olive oil. Add cream sauce and reduce heat to low. Cook 1 to 2 minutes, stirring occasionally.

Add sauce to pasta and toss to coat. Season with salt and pepper to taste. Garnish with parsley and serve immediately.

1 pound farfalle
(or gluten-free pasta)

½ cup finely chopped sun-dried tomatoes

2 tablespoons olive oil

1 large onion, chopped

4 garlic cloves, minced

½ cup raw cashews or blanched almonds*

2 cups water

1 tablespoon lemon juice

2 teaspoons sea salt

1 pound sliced mushrooms

Freshly ground black pepper

Chopped fresh Italian parsley for garnish

*If you are not using a high-powered blender, such as a Vitamix, soak cashews or almonds overnight or boil for 10 minutes and drain. This will soften them and ensure a silky smooth cream.

WILD MUSHROOM RIGATONI
RIGATONI AI FUNGHI SELVATICI

SERVES 4 TO 6

This ultra-elegant dish is perfect for mushroom lovers of any age. Creamy, comforting, and dinner-party chic.

½ ounce dried wild mushrooms

1 cup warm water

1 pound rigatoni

3 tablespoons olive oil

1 onion, finely chopped

8 ounces fresh mushrooms (shiitake, cremini, or a mix), sliced

3 garlic cloves, minced

1 teaspoon sea salt

½ cup white wine

¼ cup all-purpose flour

2 cups almond or soy milk

¾ cup chopped sun-dried tomatoes (optional)

Freshly ground black pepper

Chopped fresh Italian parsley for garnish

Reconstitute dried mushrooms in warm water according to package directions. Drain and set aside.

Bring a large pot of salted water to a boil. Add rigatoni and cook according to package directions. Drain and return to the pot.

Meanwhile, in a large skillet, heat 1 tablespoon of the oil over medium-high heat. Add onion, fresh mushrooms, and reconstituted dried mushrooms, and let cook until soft. Add garlic and salt, and let cook for 1 minute more, until fragrant. Add wine and let bubble down for a few minutes until reduced by half. Transfer mushroom mixture to a bowl and set aside, reserving the skillet. Add the remaining 2 tablespoons oil to reserved skillet and heat over medium heat. Add flour and whisk with a spatula for a few minutes to form a roux (or paste). Add almond milk and continue to whisk until mixture comes to a boil and thickens. Add reserved mushroom mixture to the skillet and let cook for another minute. Add sun-dried tomatoes, if using.

Add sauce to pasta and toss to coat. Season with pepper. Top with parsley and serve.

PENNE WITH SUN-DRIED TOMATO CREAM SAUCE*

PENNE CON CREMA DI POMODORI SECCHI

SERVES 4 TO 6

If there was such a thing as fine-dining comfort food, this would be it! It's addictive and crave-inducing like macaroni and cheese, but it's elegant and classy with the slick penne and flecks of sun-dried tomatoes. Fit for all occasions, this will be your new "it" pasta. If serving for spice lovers, you can be a little more generous with your "pinch" of red pepper flakes.

NOTE: If sauce thickens too much as it sits, reconstitute the pasta by adding a little bit of nondairy milk. Stir over medium heat until smooth. Adjust seasoning again to taste.

1 pound penne
(or gluten-free pasta)

1 cup chopped sun-dried tomatoes

3 tablespoons olive oil

⅓ cup all-purpose flour (or gluten-free all-purpose flour)

3½ cups almond milk

¼ cup nutritional yeast flakes

2 tablespoons tomato paste

2 teaspoons sea salt

1 teaspoon garlic powder

1 teaspoon dried basil

Pinch of crushed red pepper

Bring a large pot of salted water to a boil. Add penne and cook according to package directions. Right before draining, add ½ cup of the sun-dried tomatoes to the boiling water. Drain and return to the pot.

Meanwhile, in a medium saucepan, make a roux (or paste) by whisking the oil and flour over medium heat for 3 to 5 minutes. Then add almond milk, nutritional yeast, tomato paste, salt, garlic powder, basil, and red pepper to the saucepan and bring to a boil, whisking frequently. Reduce heat to low, add the remaining ½ cup sun-dried tomatoes, and let simmer until the sauce thickens. Transfer to a blender and blend until smooth. Add sauce to pasta, and toss to coat. Season to taste and serve immediately.

PASTA ALLA NORMA WITH RICOTTA*
PASTA ALLA NORMA CON RICOTTA SALATA

SERVES 4 TO 6

Pasta alla Norma is pasta in tomato sauce with sautéed eggplant. This Sicilian staple is hearty and easy to whip up, and every time I make it for company, the guests always ask for the recipe. The secret ingredient is a tablespoon of brown sugar and drizzle of balsamic vinegar to brighten the flavor of the tomatoes and soften the acidity.

Generously salt the cubed eggplant and place in a colander. Let sit and sweat for about 15 minutes. Rinse and blot the eggplant with paper towels or a dry kitchen towel to remove excess moisture and salt.

Heat oil in a medium saucepan over medium-high heat. Add eggplant and cook until lightly browned, 5 to 7 minutes. Reduce heat to medium and cook about 15 minutes until very soft and tender. Add garlic and red pepper and let cook for 1 minute more. Add crushed tomatoes and brown sugar. Cook and stir for a few more minutes. Season with black pepper.

Meanwhile, bring a large pot of salted water to a boil. Add rigatoni and cook according to package directions. Drain and return to the pot.

Add sauce to pasta and toss to coat. Divide among bowls, and drizzle each portion with vinegar. Top with basil and a few tablespoons of ricotta. Serve immediately.

Sea salt

2 medium eggplants, cut into ½-inch cubes

3 tablespoons olive oil

3 garlic cloves, minced

¼ teaspoon crushed red pepper

1 (28-ounce) can crushed tomatoes

1 tablespoon brown sugar

Freshly ground black pepper

1 pound rigatoni (or gluten-free pasta)

Balsamic vinegar for drizzling

¼ cup fresh basil

Rockin' Ricotta (page 242)

CREAMY YELLOW PEPPER PASTA
FARFALLE CON CREMA DI PEPERONI

SERVES 4 TO 6

This (no longer) top-secret recipe came straight from Lecce, Italy, from my Italian nonna, Lina, translated by her kids Lele and Danielle. It is bowtie pasta tossed with cream sauce made with blended roasted yellow bell peppers (with one red bell pepper for color), capers, onions, and a touch of olive oil. So fresh, authentic, and "accidentally" vegan!

NOTE: If sauce thickens too much as it sits, reconstitute the pasta by adding a little water or non-dairy milk. Stir over medium heat until smooth. Adjust seasoning again to taste.

3 yellow bell peppers

1 red bell pepper

1 pound bowtie pasta (or gluten-free pasta)

3 tablespoons olive oil, plus extra for drizzling

1 large onion, chopped

1¾ teaspoons sea salt

1 garlic clove

1 tablespoon drained capers

⅛ teaspoon crushed red pepper

Freshly ground black pepper

Parmesan Topping (page 244)

Using tongs, place peppers directly on the open flame of a stovetop gas burner or grill and roast, turning frequently to make sure all sides are black. Once each pepper is completely charred, place in a brown paper bag and roll the top of the bag to seal and let pepper steam. Let sit 15 minutes. Remove peppers from bag and peel away blackened skin. Remove stem and seeds.

Meanwhile, bring a large pot of salted water to a boil. Add bowties and cook according to package directions. Drain and return to the pot.

In a medium skillet, heat 1 tablespoon of the oil over medium-high heat and add onion. Season with salt and cook until soft.

In a blender (not a food processor), combine roasted pepper flesh, onion, garlic, the remaining 2 tablespoons oil, salt, and capers. Blend until very smooth.

Add sauce and crushed red pepper to pasta, and toss to coat. Season with salt and pepper, and distribute into bowls. Sprinkle each serving with Parmesan topping and a very light drizzle of olive oil.

FUSILLI WITH MINTED EGGPLANT SAUCE*

FUSILLI CON SUGO DI MELANZANE E MENTA

SERVES 4 TO 6

I've served this pasta to so many eggplant haters who surprisingly go back for seconds. The eggplant is roasted and pureed to creamy perfection with sun-dried tomatoes and fresh mint. It's sweet, creamy, with a touch of tang! You can serve leftovers the next day as a cold pasta salad.

NOTE: If sauce thickens too much as it sits, reconstitute the pasta by adding a little water or non-dairy milk. Stir over medium heat until smooth. Adjust seasoning again to taste.

Preheat the oven to 400°F.

Cut off the stem end and bottom end of each eggplant, then cut in half, lengthwise. Score the flesh of each half with a knife by making a few diagonal lines one way, then a few diagonal lines the other way. Cut deep into the flesh, but do not cut the skin. Lightly brush the flesh with oil and place, flat side down, on a large baking sheet. Roast for 40 minutes. Let cool slightly.

Meanwhile, bring a large pot of salted water to a boil. Add fusilli and cook according to package directions. Drain and return to pot.

Using a large spoon, scoop out the flesh of the eggplant and discard skins. Make the sauce by combining eggplant flesh, the ½ cup oil, water, lemon juice, brown sugar, red pepper, salt, and pepper in a food processor. Process until smooth. Add sun-dried tomatoes and pulse a few more times. Pieces of sun-dried tomatoes will remain.

Add sauce and mint to pasta, and toss to coat. Add salt to taste and serve.

2 medium eggplants

½ cup olive oil, plus extra for brushing

1 pound fusilli (or gluten-free pasta)

½ cup water

1 tablespoon lemon juice

1 tablespoon brown sugar

½ teaspoon crushed red pepper

2¼ teaspoons sea salt

½ teaspoon freshly ground black pepper

¾ cup chopped sun-dried tomatoes

½ cup chopped fresh mint

TEQUILA TEMPEH FETTUCCINE *

FETTUCCINE AL TEMPEH SALTATE CON TEQUILA

SERVES 4 TO 6

I can't say that either tequila or tempeh is Italian, but this recipe has been with the Coscarellis for years! Italian or not, this tipsy pasta is a real showstopper.

NOTE: If sauce thickens too much as it sits, reconstitute the pasta by adding a little nondairy milk. Stir over medium heat until smooth. Adjust seasoning again to taste.

½ cup raw cashews or blanched almonds*

1½ cups water

3 tablespoons olive oil

1 (8-ounce) package tempeh, thinly sliced

¾ cup water

¼ cup soy sauce

1 red bell pepper, thinly sliced

1 yellow bell pepper, thinly sliced

½ red onion, thinly sliced

4 garlic cloves, minced

½ jalapeño pepper, minced (seeds and veins removed)

½ cup vegetable broth

¼ cup gold tequila

2 tablespoons lime juice

2 teaspoons agave

1½ teaspoons sea salt

1 pound spinach fettuccine or linguine (or gluten-free pasta)

½ cup chopped fresh cilantro

*If you are not using a high-powered blender, such as a Vitamix, soak cashews or almonds overnight or boil for 10 minutes and drain. This will soften them and ensure a silky smooth cream.

In a blender, combine cashews and water. Process on high until very smooth, about 2 minutes. Set aside.

Heat 1 tablespoon of the oil in a medium skillet over medium-high heat, and cook tempeh until lightly browned on both sides. Add more oil if needed. Add water and soy sauce, and let bubble down until a very thick glaze forms.

In a separate large skillet, heat the remaining 2 tablespoons oil over medium heat and sauté peppers and onion. Let cook, stirring occasionally, until vegetables are soft, for 10 to 15 minutes. Add garlic, jalapeño, broth, tequila, lime juice, agave, salt, tempeh mixture, and cashew cream. Bring to a gentle boil and let reduce slightly, about 5 minutes. Adjust seasoning, and if tequila taste is too strong, let simmer a little more.

Meanwhile, bring a large pot of salted water to a boil. Add fettuccine and cook according to package directions. Drain and return to the pot.

Add sauce to pasta and toss to coat. Adjust seasoning to taste, and let sit for 5 to 10 minutes to allow sauce to thicken. If sauce thickens too much as it sits, add more broth as needed. Stir in cilantro and serve immediately.

YOU-WON'T-BE-SINGLE-FOR-LONG PASTA CARBONARA WITH SHIITAKE BACON*
PASTA ALLA CARBONARA CON PANCETTA DI SHIITAKE

SERVES 4 TO 6

As if carbonara isn't lovable enough for having the word "carb" in it, here's another reason to make it your favorite pasta. The creamy, indulgent sauce is made from healthy, high-protein tofu, but it tastes like it has all sorts of dairy products in it. Top it with shiitake bacon (simply thinly sliced roasted shiitake mushrooms with olive oil and sea salt) and it's the perfect bait for your long-term mate!

NOTE: If sauce thickens too much as it sits, reconstitute the pasta by adding a little water or non-dairy milk. Stir over medium heat until smooth. Adjust seasoning again to taste.

For the shiitake bacon: Preheat the oven to 375°F.

On a large rimmed baking sheet, toss mushrooms with oil, salt, and pepper. Bake for about 30 minutes, turning frequently with a spatula, until lightly browned and crisp.

For the pasta: Bring a large pot of salted water to a boil. Add pasta and cook according to package directions. Drain and return to the pot.

Meanwhile, heat oil in a medium skillet over medium heat. Add onion and let cook until soft. Add garlic and let cook a few more minutes. Remove from heat.

In a blender, combine onion, garlic, tofu, water, lemon juice, and salt. Process on high until very smooth, about 2 minutes.

Add sauce to pasta and toss to coat. Season with pepper and add more salt to taste. Let pasta sit for about 5 minutes to allow sauce to thicken slightly. Top with shiitake bacon, parsley, Parmesan topping, if using, and serve.

SHIITAKE BACON

1 pound shiitake mushrooms, trimmed and thinly sliced (about ¼ inch thick)

¼ cup olive oil

1¼ teaspoons sea salt

½ teaspoon freshly ground black pepper

PASTA CARBONARA

1 pound long pasta (spaghetti, linguine, fettuccine) (or gluten-free pasta)

2 tablespoons olive oil

1 large onion, chopped

3 garlic cloves, minced

14 ounces soft tofu

½ cup water

2 tablespoons lemon juice

2½ teaspoons sea salt

Freshly ground black pepper

Chopped fresh Italian parsley for garnish

Parmesan Topping (page 244), optional

PESTO MAC 'N' CHEESE*
MACCHERONI AL FORNO CON FORMAGGIO E PESTO

SERVES 4 TO 6

If you love pesto and you love mac 'n' cheese, this is a guaranteed home run. My recipe tester Ann Marie made it for her son Matthew and he licked his bowl clean. Funny thing is, when I make this for adults, they also lick their bowls clean. Be sure to save a bowl for yourself!

1 pound elbow macaroni
(or gluten-free pasta)

3 tablespoons olive oil

⅓ cup all-purpose flour
(or gluten-free flour)

2 garlic cloves, minced

3 cups almond or soy milk

½ cup nutritional yeast flakes

2 tablespoons tomato paste

2 teaspoons sea salt

1 tablespoon lemon juice

Classic Pesto Sauce (page 233)

Bring a large pot of salted water to a boil. Add macaroni and cook according to package directions. Drain and return to the pot.

Meanwhile, in a medium saucepan, make a roux (or paste) by whisking the oil and flour over medium heat for 3 to 5 minutes. Add garlic and let cook for 1 minute more. Then add nondairy milk, nutritional yeast, tomato paste, and salt to the saucepan and bring to a boil, whisking frequently. Reduce heat to low and let simmer until the sauce thickens. Adjust seasoning to taste and stir in lemon juice.

Add sauce to pasta and toss to coat. Divide among serving bowls. Top each portion with a dollop of pesto sauce and allow guests to mix it in as they eat.

CHI DICE MALE DEI MACCHERONI È UN FESSO.
(WHO SPEAKS BADLY OF MACARONI IS A FOOL.)

PASTA IN PINK SAUCE
PASTA CON LA SALSA ROSA

SERVES 4 TO 6

Pink is my favorite color to wear, so naturally, pink sauce is my favorite sauce to eat. Who could say no to a savory tomato sauce with a touch of cream? Not this girl!

NOTE: If sauce thickens too much as it sits, reconstitute the pasta by adding a little nondairy milk. Stir over medium heat until smooth. Adjust seasoning again to taste.

1 pound bucatini or thick spaghetti (or gluten-free pasta)

2 tablespoons olive oil

3 garlic cloves, minced

1 (28-ounce) can crushed tomatoes

2 teaspoons sea salt

2 teaspoons sugar

½ cup raw cashews*

½ cup water

½ cup chopped fresh basil, plus extra for garnish, cut into chiffonade, see Tip (page 26)

*If you are not using a high-powered blender, such as a Vitamix, soak cashews overnight or boil for 10 minutes and drain. This will soften them and ensure a silky smooth cream.

Bring a large pot of salted water to a boil. Add bucatini and cook according to package directions. Drain and return to the pot.

Heat oil in a large saucepan over medium heat. Add garlic and cook about 1 minute. Stir in tomatoes, salt, and sugar. Let cook over medium-low heat for 10 minutes, stirring occasionally.

In the meantime, combine cashews and water in a blender. Process on high until very smooth, about 2 minutes. Stir cashew cream into the tomato sauce and turn off heat. Stir in basil and toss with hot pasta. Garnish with basil chiffonade and serve immediately.

PENNE PUTTANESCA

PENNE ALLA PUTTANESCA

SERVES 4 TO 6

Put that puttanesca on the dinner table and watch it get gobbled up in minutes! This recipe is intensely flavorful and comes together in only ten minutes. Who needs anchovies when you've got capers?

1 pound penne
(or gluten-free pasta)

2 tablespoons olive oil

4 garlic cloves, minced

1 (28-ounce) can diced tomatoes

½ cup kalamata olives, chopped

2 tablespoons drained capers

1 teaspoon sea salt

¼ teaspoon crushed red pepper

Freshly ground black pepper

¼ cup chopped fresh Italian parsley

Parmesan Topping (page 244), optional

Bring a large pot of salted water to a boil. Add penne and cook according to package directions. Drain and return to the pot.

Meanwhile, heat oil in a large skillet over medium heat. Add garlic and let cook 1 minute until fragrant. Add tomatoes, olives, capers, salt, and red pepper. Season with black pepper, and simmer for 10 minutes.

Add sauce and parsley to pasta, and toss to coat. Season to taste and serve. If desired, serve with Parmesan topping.

WHOLE WHEAT SPAGHETTI WITH MUSHROOMS
SPAGHETTI INTEGRALI AI FUNGHI

SERVES 4 TO 6

Years ago in Italy, peasants would use bread crumbs on top of pasta instead of Parmesan cheese. Now the trend has caught on and restaurants do it as a novelty. It's a perfect trick for vegans and is my favorite way to top off spaghetti with mushrooms. The key to whole wheat pasta is to cook it thoroughly (not al dente), so that it is pleasant to chew.

Bring a large pot of salted water to a boil. Add spaghetti and cook according to package directions. Reserve ½ cup of the cooking water, then drain and return pasta to the pot.

Meanwhile, in a large skillet, heat oil over medium-high heat and add garlic. Cook for 1 minute until fragrant. Add mushrooms and salt, and let cook until mushrooms are soft and lightly browned. Season with pepper. Add broth and wine, and let simmer until reduced by half.

Add mushroom mixture to pasta and toss with reserved pasta water and parsley. Drizzle with more oil, if needed, and season to taste. Divide into bowls and sprinkle each portion with bread crumbs.

1 package whole wheat spaghetti (12 to 16 ounces)

¼ cup olive oil, plus extra for drizzling

6 garlic cloves, minced

1½ pounds mixed mushrooms, thinly sliced

1 teaspoon sea salt

Freshly ground black pepper

½ cup vegetable broth

½ cup white wine

½ cup chopped fresh Italian parsley

Toasted Bread Crumbs (page 244)

POTATO GNOCCHI IN HERB-GARLIC SAUCE
GNOCCHI CON SALSA ALLE ERBE AROMATICHE

SERVES 4

MAKE-AHEAD TIP: You can make the dough or uncooked cut gnocchi the day before and store it in the refrigerator. You could also freeze the cut gnocchi and boil before serving.

1 large russet potato (14 to 16 ounces), peeled and cut into 2-inch pieces

1¼ cups all-purpose flour, plus extra for rolling

½ teaspoon sea salt

¼ teaspoon ground nutmeg

¼ teaspoon freshly ground black pepper

2 tablespoons olive oil, plus more as needed

1 garlic clove, minced

½ teaspoon dried basil

½ teaspoon dried oregano

Parmesan Topping (page 244)

Chopped fresh Italian parsley for garnish

Place potato pieces in a large pot and cover with cold water. Cover and bring to a boil. Cook until potatoes are fork-tender. Drain and return to the pot. Pass potatoes through a potato ricer, or thoroughly mash the potatoes while they are still warm. Then, transfer to a medium bowl and refrigerate until completely cool.

Add flour, salt, nutmeg, and pepper to the potatoes. Mix well with a large spoon to combine. Knead with your hands for 1 to 2 minutes until a soft, slightly sticky dough has formed. Generously flour the work surface and your hands. Working with a handful of dough at a time, roll the dough into ropes about 1 inch in diameter. Dip a sharp knife in flour and cut each rope into 1-inch-long pillows.

Fill a medium saucepan with salted water and bring to a boil. Heat oil in a large nonstick skillet over medium heat.

When the water is boiling, reduce heat to a simmer and gently drop in the gnocchi, about 20 at a time. The gnocchi will start to float in about 2 minutes. When the last gnocchi has floated to the surface, let cook for 2 minutes. Using a slotted spoon, immediately transfer the gnocchi to the skillet of oil. Add garlic, basil, and oregano. Let cook for a few minutes on each side. Add more oil and seasoning as needed. You will have to do this in several batches, until all the gnocchi is cooked. Season with salt and pepper, and sprinkle with Parmesan topping and parsley.

BUTTERNUT RAVIOLI WITH BROWN SUGAR AND CRISPY SAGE

RAVIOLI ALLA ZUCCA CON SALVIA E ZUCCHERO DI CANNA

MAKES ABOUT 20 (3-INCH) ROUND RAVIOLI

ROASTED BUTTERNUT SQUASH

12 ounces cubed butternut squash

2 tablespoons olive oil

Sea salt

FILLING

1 onion, finely chopped

¼ cup chopped pecans

½ teaspoon sea salt

Freshly ground black pepper

Homemade Ravioli Dough (page 237), rolled into thin sheets

¼ cup vegan margarine

¼ cup olive oil

1 tablespoon brown sugar, plus extra if needed

½ cup fresh sage leaves

Pinch of ground nutmeg

For the roasted butternut squash: Preheat the oven to 400°F. Spread butternut squash on a large rimmed baking sheet and toss with oil. Season with salt and roast for 45 to 50 minutes, until very tender when pierced with a fork. Remove from oven and puree in a food processor until smooth. Leave in food processor.

For the filling: In a large skillet, heat oil over medium-high heat and sauté onion until soft and lightly browned. Add pecans and let cook for 1 minute more. Transfer onion and pecans to the roasted butternut squash in the food processor. Add salt and season with pepper. Process until almost smooth and adjust seasoning to taste.

For the ravioli: Cut pasta sheets into 3-inch circles and place 1 to 2 teaspoons of filling in the center of each circle. Lightly wet edges with cold water using your fingertips, then fold in half and pinch edges to seal.

Bring a large pot filled with 2 inches of water to a gentle boil. Add ravioli and cook 3 to 5 minutes, until the pasta looks cooked. Meanwhile, in a large nonstick skillet, heat margarine and oil over medium heat until the margarine begins to bubble. Stir in brown sugar. Remove the ravioli from the water using a slotted spoon and transfer to the skillet of margarine. Add sage and let the ravioli cook, turning frequently, for a few minutes until lightly browned. Add more brown sugar, if needed. Season with nutmeg and serve immediately.

MUSHROOM WONTON RAVIOLI
RAVIOLI RIPIENI DI FUNGHI

SERVES 4

Too busy to roll your own pasta dough? Just use wonton wrappers instead! Find egg-free wonton (or gyoza) wrappers in the Asian section of your grocery store.

MAKE-AHEAD TIP: Wontons can be filled and placed on a baking sheet covered with plastic wrap and refrigerated for 24 hours. They can also be filled and frozen in a single layer, then placed in a plastic bag or Tupperware once frozen. Allow more cooking time if cooking straight from the freezer.

FILLING

1 tablespoon olive oil

8 ounces mushrooms, trimmed and sliced

3 shallots, sliced

¼ teaspoon sea salt

¼ teaspoon freshly ground black pepper

¼ cup white wine

1 teaspoon fresh thyme leaves

1 tablespoon chopped fresh Italian parsley, plus extra for garnish

1 package vegan wonton wrappers

1 cup marinara sauce

For the filling: In a medium skillet, heat oil over medium-high heat and sauté mushrooms, shallots, salt, and pepper, until mushrooms and shallots are soft and lightly browned. Add wine, reduce heat to medium-low, and let cook until it bubbles away. Turn off the heat, and mix in thyme and parsley. Adjust seasoning to taste and pulse a few times in a food processor.

For the wontons: Place the wonton wrappers on a lightly floured surface and brush each wrapper with water. Place about 1½ teaspoons of the filling near the corner of wonton and fold over carefully to make a triangle. With your fingers, enclose the filling, pressing out any air bubbles, and seal very well. Place on a lightly floured baking sheet and continue until all wrappers are filled.

Bring a medium saucepan of salted water to a boil, and turn down to a simmer. Place 4 to 6 wontons in the water and gently boil for 3 to 4 minutes. Do not boil the wontons vigorously because the wrapper will break. The wontons will rise to the surface after about 2 minutes. Continue cooking for another 2 to 3 minutes. Using a slotted spoon, lift the wontons carefully out of the water and place on a large plate. Repeat until you have cooked all the wontons.

To serve: Top the wontons with marinara sauce and garnish with parsley.

LENTIL MANICOTTI
MANICOTTI ALLE LENTICCHIE

SERVES 4 TO 6

Stuff yourself with this stuffed pasta and feel no guilt! Loaded with nutrient- and protein-rich lentils, tofu, and eggplant, this meal is great to power up when you're feeling run down or extra hungry. This can be prepared the day before and heated up before serving.

MAKE-AHEAD TIP: Unbaked manicotti can be assembled and refrigerated up to 2 days in advance until ready to bake.

Preheat the oven to 350°F. Lightly grease a large baking sheet and a 9 x 13-inch pan.

Place the eggplant on the prepared baking sheet and toss with oil. Season with salt and pepper and bake for 20 minutes, turning occasionally. Meanwhile, combine lentils and ricotta in a large bowl. Add eggplant.

Cook the manicotti noodles according to package directions. In a large bowl, stir marinara, nondairy milk, and brown sugar.

Spread a layer of the marinara sauce on the bottom of the prepared 9 x 13-inch pan.

Stuff the manicotti with the ricotta mixture as desired and place in rows in the pan. Remaining filling can be refrigerated or frozen for another use. Top with the remaining sauce covering all exposed shells. Season with salt and pepper. Cover with foil and bake for about 25 minutes until cooked through. Remove from oven and let sit for 5 minutes before serving.

1 eggplant, cut into ½-inch cubes

2 tablespoons olive oil

Sea salt

Freshly ground black pepper

1 (15-ounce) can lentils, rinsed and drained

Rockin' Ricotta (page 242)

1 (8-ounce) package manicotti

1 (26-ounce) jar marinara sauce

¼ cup soy, almond, or rice milk

2 tablespoons brown sugar or maple syrup

LASAGNA BOLOGNESE
LASAGNA ALLA BOLOGNESE

SERVES 6

Bolognese without the meat? You bet! This recipe underwent loads of testing. I'm talking thirty or forty times in one month. Yes, I was making at least one version a day for a whole month until it was perfect. I hope you love it as much as my family did when I finally hit the winning recipe. By the way, they still aren't sick of it!

MAKE-AHEAD TIP: *Unbaked lasagna can be assembled and refrigerated up to 2 days in advance until ready to bake.*

Preheat the oven to 375°F. Lightly grease a 9 x 13-inch pan.

Heat oil in a large nonstick skillet over medium-high heat. Add mushrooms and cook until almost soft. Add seitan and continue to cook until lightly browned. Add basil, red pepper, salt, and pepper. Let cook for 1 minute more. Remove from heat and transfer mixture to the food processor. Pulse about 15 times until roughly chopped.

For the sauce: Combine marinara sauce, nondairy milk, and brown sugar in a large bowl. Stir until combined.

To assemble and bake the lasagna: Spread a thin layer of sauce on the bottom of the prepared pan. Arrange 4 lasagna noodles across the pan; it's okay if they overlap a little. Spread another layer of sauce, half of the Bolognese mixture, 4 noodles, half of the ricotta, 4 noodles, sauce, the remaining Bolognese mixture, 4 noodles, the remaining ricotta, and 4 more noodles. Top with the remaining sauce.

Cover the baking pan with foil and bake for 45 minutes, or until noodles are cooked and sauce is hot and bubbling. Remove from oven and let rest for 5 minutes before serving.

2 tablespoons olive oil

8 ounces sliced mushrooms

1 (8-ounce) package seitan, sliced

1 teaspoon dried basil

¼ teaspoon crushed red pepper

1 teaspoon sea salt

1 teaspoon freshly ground black pepper

2 (26-ounce) jars marinara sauce

½ cup soy, almond, or rice milk

2 tablespoons brown sugar

1 pound no-boil lasagna noodles

Rockin' Ricotta (page 242)

WHITE LASAGNA WITH ROASTED BUTTERNUT SQUASH AND SPINACH

LASAGNA BIANCA CON ZUCCA ARROSTITA

SERVES 6

Stuck in a lasagna rut? Snap out of the usual red-sauce routine with this divine lasagna.

ROASTED BUTTERNUT SQUASH

12 ounces cubed butternut squash

2 tablespoons olive oil

Sea salt

SPINACH

1 tablespoon olive oil

5 ounces baby spinach

ALFREDO SAUCE

1 tablespoon olive oil

1 large onion, chopped

2 garlic cloves, minced

1½ cups raw cashews or blanched almonds*

3 cups water

1 tablespoon lemon juice

2 teaspoons sea salt

¼ teaspoon freshly ground black pepper

1 pound no-boil lasagna noodles

Rockin' Ricotta (page 242)

*If you are not using a high-powered blender, such as a Vitamix, soak cashews or almonds overnight or boil for 10 minutes and drain. This will soften them and ensure a silky smooth cream.

For the roasted butternut squash: Preheat the oven to 400°F. Spread butternut squash on a large rimmed baking sheet and toss with oil. Season with salt and roast for 30 minutes, until fork-tender. Remove from oven and puree in a food processor until smooth. If needed, add 1 to 2 tablespoons of water.

For the spinach: In a large skillet, heat oil over medium heat. Add spinach and let cook until just wilted.

For the Alfredo sauce: Heat oil in a medium skillet over medium-high heat. Add onion and let cook until soft. Remove from heat. In a blender, combine onion, garlic, cashews, water, lemon juice, salt, and pepper. Process on high until very smooth, about 2 minutes, and set aside.

To assemble and bake the lasagna: Preheat the oven to 375°F. Lightly grease a 9 x 13-inch pan.

Spread a thin layer of sauce on the bottom of the prepared pan. Arrange 4 lasagna noodles across the pan; it's okay if they overlap a little. Layer half the ricotta, 4 noodles, sauce, butternut squash, spinach, sauce, 4 noodles, sauce, remaining half ricotta, and 4 more noodles. Top lasagna with remaining sauce, reserving about 1 cup for serving. Noodles should be evenly coated.

Cover the baking pan with foil and bake for 50 minutes, or until noodles are cooked through. Remove from oven and let rest for 5 minutes before serving. Top each serving with a generous spoonful of heated sauce.

THE MAIN COURSE

(SECONDO PIATTI)

From risotto to polenta, grains and beans are a staple in many Italian entrées. Here I explore some of my favorites: ancient grains and seeds like farro and quinoa, and classics like Arborio rice, polenta, and chickpeas. My favorite beans are white cannellini beans because they are so plush and creamy, which is a particularly useful texture in vegan cooking!

AVOCADO BASIL QUINOA BOWL WITH CHILI OLIVE OIL

QUINOA ALL'AVOCADO CON OLIO AL PEPERONCINO

SERVES 4

This simple grain bowl is amped up with California's finest fruit and Italy's favorite herb! You can use brown rice instead of quinoa, if desired, and you can use frozen quinoa or brown rice for a shortcut. Get crazy with the add-ons for maximum flavor.

SAUCE

1 bunch fresh basil

½ cup walnuts, almonds, or cashews

2 avocados

2 tablespoons lemon juice, plus extra for drizzling

2 garlic cloves

½ cup olive oil

1½ teaspoons sea salt

½ teaspoon freshly ground black pepper

4 cups cooked quinoa (any color variety)

1 cup halved cherry tomatoes

3 scallions, trimmed and thinly sliced

Chili olive oil (page 238) or crushed red pepper flakes for serving

Optional add-ons: sliced avocado, grilled corn, sliced almonds, currants, chopped kalamata olives, or something delicious from the farmers' market

For the sauce: Combine basil, walnuts, avocados, lemon juice, garlic, oil, salt, and pepper in a food processor. Process until smooth.

To assemble the bowls: Fill each bowl with a serving of quinoa. Then top each bowl with some sauce, tomatoes, scallions, and any desired add-ons. Drizzle with lemon juice and chili oil or red pepper. Season with salt and pepper, and serve.

BAKED TEMPEH IN MUSHROOM CREAM SAUCE

TEMPEH AL FORNO SU VELLUTATA DI FUNGHI

SERVES 4

Even if you don't love tempeh, you'll love it when it's smothered in this luxurious cream sauce with mushrooms! When you're blending your cashews, make sure you blend them well until they have formed an emulsified cream sauce. Any nutty particles will ruin the dish.

In a large nonstick skillet, heat oil over medium-high heat and arrange tempeh pieces in the skillet. Using tongs or a spatula to flip the pieces, brown tempeh on each side, about 5 minutes. Transfer to a plate.

Preheat the oven to 350°F. Lightly grease a 9 x 13-inch pan.

In a blender, puree cashews, water, garlic, and salt. Transfer to a large bowl. Add thyme and scallions to the cashew cream and mix with a spoon.

In the prepared pan, arrange mushrooms and tempeh, and pour the cashew cream on top. Dust the top with paprika and cover the pan with foil. Bake for about 30 minutes, or until mushrooms are soft. Garnish with fresh thyme before serving and adjust salt to taste.

1 tablespoon olive oil

1 (8-ounce) package tempeh, thinly sliced

1 cup raw cashews*

2 cups water

3 garlic cloves

2 teaspoons sea salt

2 teaspoons fresh thyme leaves, plus extra for garnish

2 scallions, trimmed and thinly sliced

8 ounces mushrooms, sliced

Paprika for garnish

*If you are not using a high-powered blender, such as a Vitamix, soak cashews overnight or boil cashews for 10 minutes and drain. This will soften the cashews and ensure a silky smooth cream.

CHLOE'S RAWSAGNA

SERVES 4 TO 6

SUN-DRIED TOMATO SAUCE

2 cups (6 ounces) sun-dried tomatoes (dry-packed), soaked in water for at least 2 hours

1 tomato, chopped

¼ cup olive oil

2 tablespoons lemon juice

2 tablespoons maple syrup

2 teaspoons sea salt

¼ teaspoon crushed red pepper

PINE NUT RICOTTA

1½ cups (8 ounces) raw pine nuts, soaked in water for at least 1 hour

1 tablespoon lemon juice

¼ cup plus 1 tablespoon water

2 tablespoons nutritional yeast

1 teaspoon sea salt

PISTACHIO PESTO

2 cups packed fresh basil

½ cup shelled raw pistachios

¼ cup olive oil

1 tablespoon lemon juice

½ teaspoon sea salt

1 large zucchini, halved and thinly sliced with a mandoline or vegetable peeler (room temperature)

2 large heirloom tomatoes, sliced (room temperature)

Freshly ground black pepper

This dish is inspired by my favorite meal in New York City, the lasagna from Pure Food and Wine, an enchanting raw, vegan restaurant in Gramercy Park. My roommates took me there for my twenty-sixth birthday and all of us ordered the lasagna because it looked so good at the next table. We cleaned our plates and I knew I had to go home and re-create it.

MAKE-AHEAD TIP: The tomato sauce and ricotta can be made up to 3 days in advance and stored in the refrigerator. The pistachio pesto can be made the day before and covered tightly with plastic wrap in the refrigerator.

For the sun-dried tomato sauce: Combine all ingredients in a food processor. Process until smooth.

For the pine nut ricotta: Combine all ingredients in a food processor. Process until smooth.

For the pistachio pesto: Combine all ingredients in a food processor. Pulse until combined.

To assemble the lasagna: For each serving, lay 2 slices of zucchini side by side. Top with a large spoonful of tomato sauce, and a small scoop of each of the pesto and ricotta. Then layer 2 slices of tomato, a large spoonful of tomato sauce, and a small scoop of each of the pesto and ricotta. Repeat the layers as desired. Drizzle the lasagna with oil and season with salt and pepper before serving.

CREAMY POLENTA WITH ROASTED VEGETABLE RAGÙ

POLENTA CREMOSA CON RAGÙ DI VERDURE ARROSTITE

SERVES 4

MAKE-AHEAD TIP: Polenta can be stored in the refrigerator for up to 3 days in advance. Reheat, stir in a little nondairy milk to reconstitute, and adjust seasoning to taste before serving. Vegetables can be roasted a day in advance and kept refrigerated.

POLENTA

4 cups water

1 cup yellow cornmeal (medium grind)

1 teaspoon sea salt

Freshly ground black pepper

1 tablespoon fresh thyme

1 tablespoon nutritional yeast flakes

2 tablespoons olive oil

ROASTED VEGETABLE RAGÙ

1 pound mix of broccoli, cauliflower, carrots, or squash, cut into bite-size pieces

Olive oil

Sea salt

Freshly ground black pepper

1 (26-ounce) jar marinara sauce

2 garlic cloves, minced

¼ cup soy, almond, or rice milk

1 tablespoon brown sugar or maple syrup

For the polenta: In a medium saucepan, add water, cover, and bring to a boil. Add cornmeal slowly and gradually, while whisking vigorously, to avoid clumping. Reduce heat to low, and whisk in salt and pepper. Let cook on low, uncovered, while stirring frequently with a wooden spoon for 20 to 30 minutes, or until mixture is thick and grains are cooked. Remove from heat, and stir in thyme, nutritional yeast, and oil.

For the roasted vegetable ragù: Preheat the oven to 400°F.

In a large bowl, toss vegetables with enough oil to generously coat each piece. Season with salt and pepper.

Spread vegetables in one layer on a large rimmed baking sheet. Roast for 25 to 30 minutes, stirring and rotating the vegetables every 15 minutes. If they begin to dry out, add more oil and toss. Once all vegetables are fork-tender and slightly browned, remove from oven. Adjust seasoning to taste.

Meanwhile, in a large pot, heat marinara sauce and add garlic, nondairy milk, and brown sugar. Let simmer until heated through, then add roasted vegetables.

To serve: Divide polenta into bowls and top each portion with ragù.

LEMON HERB CANNELLINI BEANS
CANNELLINI ALLE ERBE E LIMONE

SERVES 2

This is a nice, easy meal for two. I make it when I'm eating with my brother because we both go nuts for the creamy lemony flavor of the white beans paired with our two favorite veggies: spinach and mashed potatoes.

NOTE: If beans get too thick as they sit, reconstitute with extra nondairy milk and adjust seasoning to taste.

For the beans: In a large skillet, heat oil over medium heat. Add garlic and Italian seasoning, and let cook for 1 minute until fragrant. Add beans, salt, nutritional yeast, and nondairy milk. Simmer for 5 minutes. Add lemon juice and add more salt to taste. If it gets too thick, add more nondairy milk.

For the spinach: In a large skillet, heat oil over medium heat. Add spinach and let cook until wilted. Season with salt and pepper.

To assemble: On each plate, serve a scoop of mashed potatoes on a bed of spinach. Then top potatoes with the beans.

BEANS

1 tablespoon olive oil

2 garlic cloves, minced

1 teaspoon Italian seasoning

1 (15-ounce) can cannellini or other white beans, rinsed and drained

½ teaspoon sea salt

¼ cup nutritional yeast flakes

¾ cup soy, almond, or rice milk, plus extra if needed

1 tablespoon lemon juice

SPINACH

1 tablespoon olive oil

1 (5-ounce) bag baby spinach

Sea salt

Freshly ground black pepper

Mashed Potatoes with Garlic and Sea Salt (page 48)

EGGPLANT PARMESAN*

PARMIGIANA DI MELANZANE

SERVES 4 TO 6

There's nothing worse than greasy eggplant Parmesan swimming in so much cheese and oil that you can't even taste the eggplant. This veganized version is light and tasty but every bit as indulgent. My Italian grandfather Don asked for seconds, so it must be legit!

3 medium eggplants (about 3¼ pounds), sliced ¼ inch thick

Sea salt

1 tablespoon olive oil, plus extra for brushing

1 onion, chopped

3 garlic cloves, minced

1 (26-ounce) jar marinara sauce

2 tablespoons brown sugar

2 tablespoons bread crumbs for sprinkling

Mozzarella Sauce (page 237)

¼ cup chopped fresh basil

Preheat the oven to broil, set to high. Lightly grease two large baking sheets.

Generously salt the eggplant and place in a colander. Let sit and sweat for about 30 minutes.

Meanwhile, prepare the tomato sauce by heating oil in a medium saucepan over medium-high heat. Add onion and cook until soft and lightly browned. Add garlic and let cook for 1 minute. Add marinara sauce and brown sugar and cook and stir for a few more minutes.

Wipe the eggplant with paper towels to remove excess moisture. Arrange the eggplant on the baking sheets and brush with oil. Broil for 4 to 6 minutes until browned on top.

Lower the oven temperature to 350°F. Lightly grease a 9 x 13-inch pan.

To assemble the casserole: Arrange half of the eggplant slices, overlapping the slices, in the bottom of the prepared pan. Sprinkle with 1 tablespoon of the bread crumbs. Layer half of the tomato sauce and half of the mozzarella sauce on top of the bread crumbs. Repeat the layers. Bake, uncovered, for 20 minutes. Top with fresh basil and serve.

TUSCAN TOFU SCRAMBLE*
TOFU ALLA TOSCANA

SERVES 4

After ten years of being vegan, I've eaten a lot of tofu scramble—buckets and buckets if you add it all up. My hand to the tofu gods, this version is absolutely the best. The addition of sweet sun-dried tomatoes and fresh basil really takes it up a notch, making it impressive even to Level 7 tofu scramblers.

In a large nonstick skillet, heat oil over medium-high heat. Add onion, mushrooms, and 1 teaspoon of the salt. Let cook until soft and lightly browned. Add pepper, turmeric, onion powder, and garlic powder, and let cook for 1 minute, until fragrant. Add tofu, sun-dried tomatoes, nutritional yeast, and the remaining ½ teaspoon salt. Let cook until heated through and adjust seasoning to taste. Mix in basil and serve with sliced avocado or red pepper, if desired.

2 tablespoons olive oil

1 onion, chopped

8 ounces mushrooms, sliced

1½ teaspoons sea salt

½ teaspoon freshly ground black pepper

½ teaspoon turmeric

½ teaspoon onion powder

½ teaspoon garlic powder

1 (14-ounce) package firm tofu, crumbled

¼ cup finely chopped sun-dried tomatoes

1 tablespoon nutritional yeast flakes

¾ cup fresh basil, chopped

Sliced avocado (optional)

Crushed red pepper (optional)

GRILLED PORTOBELLO STEAK IN LEMON PARSLEY PESTO

PORTOBELLO GRIGLIATO CON PESTO DI PREZZEMOLO E LIMONE

SERVES 4

The art of a portobello steak is all in the sauce. In this case, the fresh and tangy lemon parsley pesto really makes the juices in the portobello come alive! This dish is best served with a grain or risotto, or on top of a mountain of Mashed Potatoes with Garlic and Sea Salt (page 48).

MAKE-AHEAD TIP: Pesto can be made the day before and stored in the refrigerator.

6 large portobello mushrooms, trimmed and cut into ½-inch slices

¼ cup olive oil, plus extra for brushing

Sea salt

Freshly ground black pepper

2 tablespoons water

1 tablespoon lemon juice

4 tablespoons drained capers

½ cup fresh Italian parsley

1 garlic clove

Preheat a grill or grill pan.

Brush mushrooms with oil on both sides and season with salt and pepper. Grill until tender and nice grill marks appear. Be sure to flip and cook each side.

In a blender or food processor, combine water, lemon juice, capers, parsley, and garlic, and process until almost smooth.

Arrange mushrooms on a platter and drizzle with sauce to serve.

ITALIAN MEATLOAF

POLPETTONE

SERVES 4

If you've been scarred from memories of frozen TV dinner meatloaf, this gourmet vegan version is surely the cure! This hearty, flavorful family meal can be served with a heaping of Mashed Potatoes with Garlic and Sea Salt (page 48).

NOTE: To start the recipe, you must cook the rice first. For a shortcut, buy frozen brown rice.

MAKE-AHEAD TIP: The rice can be made the day before or the entire meatloaf can be assembled baked or unbaked the day before.

Preheat the oven to 350°F. Brush an 8-inch square pan with oil.

In the meantime, heat the oil over medium-high heat in a large skillet and sauté onion and eggplant until soft and lightly browned and vegetables have reduced in size. If vegetables begin to stick, add a little water to the skillet. Stir in garlic and let cook for 1 minute, until fragrant. Transfer to a large bowl and add beans, rice, tomato, bread crumbs, vegetable broth, salt, pepper, and basil. Mix and mash the mixture with a large spoon until the mixture holds together. Adjust seasoning to taste.

Transfer the mixture into the prepared pan and pack it down very firmly using the back of a large spoon. It is important to pack it firmly so that it holds together while baking. In a small bowl or measuring cup, mix tomato sauce and brown sugar. Pour the tomato sauce on top of the meatloaf and cover the top of the loaf pan with foil.

Bake for 40 minutes, covered, then remove foil, and bake for an additional 20 minutes. Remove from oven and let rest for 10 minutes before serving.

2 tablespoons olive oil, plus extra for brushing

1 onion, finely chopped

1 small eggplant, diced into ½-inch cubes

4 garlic cloves, minced

1 (15-ounce) can white beans, rinsed and drained

1 cup cooked brown rice, warm

1 tomato, roughly chopped

½ cup Italian bread crumbs

¼ cup vegetable broth

1½ teaspoons sea salt

1 teaspoon freshly ground black pepper

1 teaspoon dried basil

1 (8-ounce) can tomato sauce

2 tablespoons brown sugar

WHITE WINE RISOTTO WITH SHIITAKE MUSHROOMS AND PEAS

RISOTTO AL VINO BIANCO CON FUNGHI SHIITAKE E PISELLI

SERVES 4

This velvety, plush risotto is elegant and tastes almost buttery. There's no combo like peas and mushrooms, especially with a splash of white wine. Luckily, there's no need to conceal such a lovely flavor profile with a pile of cheese. One bite and you'll forever keep your risotto vegan!

6 cups vegetable broth

3 tablespoons olive oil

1 onion, finely chopped

8 ounces shiitake mushrooms, trimmed and thinly sliced

2 garlic cloves, minced

1 cup Arborio rice

½ cup dry white wine

½ cup frozen peas, thawed

¼ cup chopped fresh Italian parsley

¾ teaspoon sea salt

Freshly ground black pepper

In a medium saucepan, heat the broth to a simmer, and let it simmer while preparing the recipe.

Heat a large nonstick skillet over medium-high heat and add oil. Reduce heat to medium high, and sauté onion and mushrooms until soft. Add garlic and let cook for 1 minute, until fragrant. Stir in rice and wine and let cook until most of the liquid evaporates.

Stir in 1 cup of the broth, and reduce heat so that mixture simmers. Stir often, cooking until most of the liquid has been absorbed by the rice. Repeat with another cup of broth, and continue stirring, adding broth 1 cup at a time, until the rice is tender (about 25 minutes).

Stir in peas, parsley, and salt. Season with pepper and stir until mixture is hot. Add more salt to taste and serve.

PUMPKIN RISOTTO
RISOTTO ALLA ZUCCA

SERVES 4

Take heart, here's a reason not to cry over summer ending. Grab yourself a can of organic pumpkin and a bag of Arborio rice, and voilà, the finest risotto in town!

5 cups vegetable broth

3 tablespoons olive oil

1 onion, finely chopped

1 large garlic clove, minced

1 cup Arborio rice

1 cup canned pumpkin puree

1 teaspoon sea salt

⅛ teaspoon nutmeg

Freshly ground black pepper

1 tablespoon chopped
fresh sage

In a medium saucepan, heat the broth to a simmer, and let it simmer while preparing the recipe.

Heat a large nonstick skillet over medium-high heat and add oil. Reduce the heat, and sauté onion until soft. Add garlic and let cook for 1 minute, until fragrant.

Stir in rice and 1 cup of the broth, and reduce heat so the mixture simmers. Stir often, cooking until most of the liquid has been absorbed by the rice. Repeat with another cup of broth, and continue stirring, adding broth 1 cup at a time, until the rice is tender (about 20 minutes).

Stir in pumpkin, salt, and nutmeg. Season with pepper and stir until mixture is hot. Stir in sage.

TEMPEH WITH 40 CLOVES OF GARLIC
TEMPEH CON 40 SPICCHI DI AGLIO

SERVES 4

You'd be surprised to know that after using forty cloves of garlic, you still won't have a trace of garlic breath! Why? Because the whole garlic cloves are cooked and braised in vegetable broth until they are mellow and sweet. Tempeh, made from fermented soy and high in protein, has a delicious nutty texture.

NOTE: For a shortcut, use store-bought peeled garlic cloves. You can also use just half the amount.

In a small bowl, whisk broth and mustard. Set aside.

In a large nonstick skillet, heat oil over medium-high heat and arrange tempeh pieces and garlic cloves in the skillet. Using tongs or a spatula, flip the tempeh and garlic cloves to cook on each side, about 5 minutes, or until nicely browned. If tempeh or garlic get too brown, lower heat.

Very carefully and slowly, add broth to the skillet. Add thyme and salt, and season with pepper. Reduce the heat to medium and let the broth bubble down until thick (about 10 minutes).

Remove from heat and add lemon juice. Mix in parsley and margarine until melted. Serve with mashed potatoes or steamed brown rice.

1½ cups vegetable broth

2 tablespoons Dijon mustard

2 tablespoons olive oil

1 (8-ounce) package tempeh, thinly sliced

40 garlic cloves, peeled and left whole (store-bought peeled garlic cloves is the way to go!)

2 teaspoons fresh thyme

½ teaspoon sea salt

Freshly ground black pepper

Juice of half a lemon

1 tablespoon chopped fresh Italian parsley

1 tablespoon vegan margarine

ROSEMARY LENTILS WITH ROASTED TOMATOES AND GARLICKY BROCCOLINI

LENTICCHIE AL ROSMARINO CON POMODORI ARROSTITI E BROCCOLINI ALL'AGLIO

SERVES 6

For the rosemary lentils: In a large pot, heat oil over medium-high heat and add onions. Let cook until soft and lightly browned. Add garlic and let cook 1 minute, until fragrant. Add curry powder, rosemary, salt, lentils, tomatoes, and broth. Bring to a boil, cover, and let simmer for about 40 minutes until lentils are tender. Stir in lemon juice and brown sugar.

For the roasted tomatoes: Preheat the oven to 400°F. On a large baking sheet, spread tomatoes, cut side up, and drizzle with oil. Add salt, garlic, and thyme. Roast for 1 hour, stirring occasionally with a spatula.

For the broccolini: Bring a large pot of salted water to a boil. Add broccolini and boil until fork-tender, 3 to 5 minutes. Drain, plunge into a large bowl of ice water, and drain again. In a large nonstick skillet, heat oil over medium-high heat and add broccolini, garlic, and nutmeg. Season with salt and pepper and sauté until lightly browned.

To serve: Place a few pieces of broccolini, roasted tomatoes, and a serving of lentils on each plate.

ROSEMARY LENTILS

1 tablespoon olive oil

2 onions, finely chopped

3 garlic cloves, minced

2 teaspoons mild curry powder

1 tablespoon chopped fresh rosemary

2 teaspoons sea salt

1 cup red or green dried lentils

1 (28-ounce) can crushed tomatoes

2 cups vegetable broth

1 tablespoon lemon juice

1 tablespoon brown sugar

ROASTED TOMATOES

4 plum tomatoes, halved

3 tablespoons olive oil

1 teaspoon sea salt

3 garlic cloves, unpeeled

⅓ bunch fresh thyme

GARLICKY BROCCOLINI

1 bunch broccolini, cut into 2-inch pieces

1 tablespoon olive oil

2 garlic cloves, minced

Pinch of ground nutmeg

Sea salt

Freshly ground black pepper

THYME FOR STUFFED PORTOBELLOS WITH ROSEMARY GRAVY*
FUNGHI PORTOBELLO RIPIENI DI TIMO E SUGHETTO AL ROSMARINO

SERVES 6

2 tablespoons olive oil

1 onion, finely chopped

1 cup cashews

4 garlic cloves, minced

1 cup cooked brown rice

1 (15-ounce) can lentils, rinsed and drained (or 2 cups cooked)

¼ cup bread crumbs

½ cup vegetable broth

1 teaspoon dried basil

1 tablespoon fresh thyme leaves, plus extra for garnish

1 teaspoon sea salt

1 teaspoon freshly ground black pepper

6 portobello mushrooms, stems and gills removed

1 tomato, sliced thinly

ROSEMARY GRAVY

2 tablespoons canola oil

1 large onion, roughly chopped

¼ cup nutritional yeast flakes

½ cup all-purpose flour

2 cups water

3 tablespoons soy sauce

1 garlic clove, minced

1 tablespoon chopped fresh rosemary

Sea salt and freshly ground black pepper

Preheat the oven to 350°F. Lightly grease a medium baking sheet.

In large skillet, heat 2 tablespoons of the oil over medium-high heat and add onion and cashews. Sauté until onion is soft and lightly browned. Add garlic and let cook a few more minutes until fragrant.

In a large bowl, combine onion mixture, brown rice, lentils, bread crumbs, broth, basil, thyme, salt, and pepper.

Brush both sides of mushroom caps with oil and season with salt and pepper. Place them top side down on baking sheet. Stuff mushrooms with about ½ cup of the lentil stuffing, and press 1 tomato slice on top of the stuffing.

Bake for about 30 minutes, or until the stuffing is browned and mushrooms are cooked through. Garnish with extra thyme and serve with gravy.

For the rosemary gravy: In a medium saucepan, heat oil over medium-high heat and sauté onion until soft. Add nutritional yeast and flour, and whisk for about 2 minutes. The mixture will be dry. Add water, soy sauce, garlic, and rosemary. Continue to cook, whisking continuously, until mixture is very thick. Transfer gravy to a blender and puree until smooth. Season to taste.

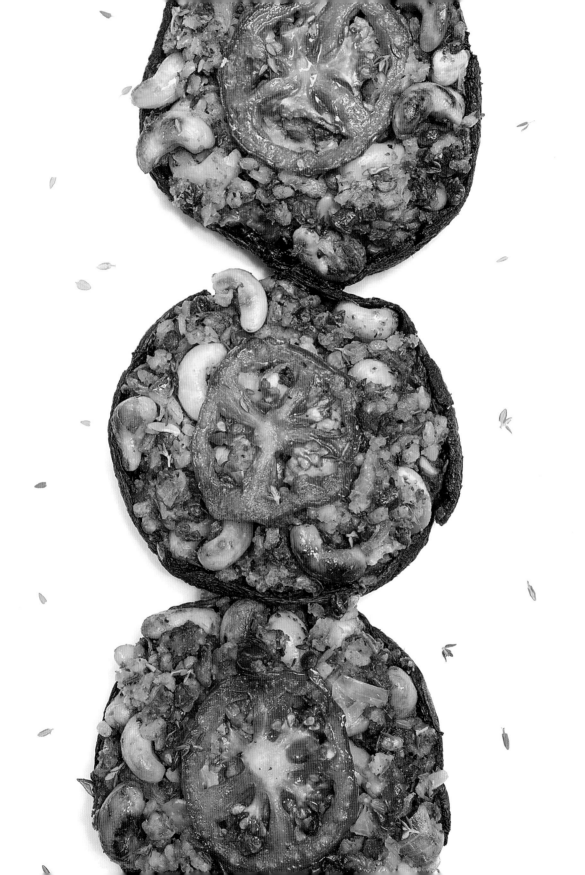

WILD MUSHROOM FARRO WITH LEMON, MINT, AND ARTICHOKES *
FARRO AI FUNGHI SELVATICI CON LIMONE, MENTA E CARCIOFI

SERVES 4 AS AN ENTRÉE; 6 TO 8 AS A SIDE

Farro is an ancient grain that is whole and nutritious with a puffy toothsome bite, similar to barley. If you don't have farro, you can use brown rice, and for a cheaper grocery list, stick to cremini or white mushrooms. This recipe is aromatic and refreshing, making it the perfect summer side or main dish.

3 tablespoons olive oil

12 to 16 ounces mixed mushrooms (shiitake, cremini, oyster, etc.), sliced

Sea salt

Freshly ground black pepper

1 (14-ounce) can artichoke hearts, drained and roughly chopped

1 garlic clove, minced

¼ cup white wine

¼ cup vegetable broth

2 cups cooked farro

2 tablespoons finely chopped fresh mint

Zest of 1 lemon

In a large skillet, heat 2 tablespoons of the oil over medium-high heat and sauté mushrooms. Season with salt and pepper and let cook until soft and lightly browned. Add artichoke hearts and cook a few more minutes. Add garlic and let cook for 1 minute, until fragrant.

Add wine and let reduce until liquid almost evaporates. Add broth and farro, and season again with salt and pepper. Let cook in pan until heated through and most of the liquid is absorbed.

Remove from heat and mix in mint and lemon zest. Drizzle with the remaining 1 tablespoon oil and serve.

DESSERTS
(DOLCI)

Dessert, my favorite part of any meal! Classic Italian dessert recipes are *far* from vegan, as they use a lot of cream, eggs, cream, and did I mention cream? So I've taken my favorite flavors and ingredients from Italian dessert (espresso, dark chocolate, lemon, rosemary, thyme, cherry, almond, and so on) and incorporated them into purely vegan recipes that are easy to make, and just as sinfully delicious as the classics (without the cream!).

CHOCOLATE-DIPPED ALMOND BISCOTTI
CANTUCCI ALLE MANDORLE RICOPERTI DI CIOCCOLATO

MAKES 8 LARGE BISCOTTI

When I was in culinary school at the Natural Gourmet Institute, we were given a biscotti assignment during our cookie unit. While all the other students followed recipes for "sesame anise" or "plain" biscotti, I decided to be the rebel of the class, throw in some orange zest, dip them in chocolate, and roll them in toasted almonds. All the students and teachers went nuts for it, and today the recipe is yours to keep!

BISCOTTI

¾ cup blanched slivered or sliced almonds

½ cup all-purpose flour*

¼ teaspoon baking powder

¼ teaspoon salt

2 tablespoons vegan margarine or coconut oil, melted

¼ cup maple syrup

½ teaspoon pure vanilla extract

1 teaspoon orange zest

TOPPING

1 cup semisweet chocolate chips (dairy-free), melted

1 cup finely chopped toasted almonds

*For a gluten-free alternative, substitute gluten-free all-purpose flour plus ⅛ teaspoon xanthan gum and see page 257).

Preheat the oven to 350°F. Line a baking sheet with parchment paper.

In a food processor, combine almonds, flour, baking powder, and salt. Process until almonds are ground and the consistency is a fine meal. Add melted margarine, maple syrup, vanilla, and orange zest, and process a little more until just combined. Do not overprocess. Dough will be wet and sticky.

Divide the dough into two equal parts on the prepared baking sheet and shape each part into a rectangle, approximately 2 x 4 inches long and about 1 inch high. If dough is too soft to form, chill in the refrigerator until easy to work with. Dip your fingers in a little cold water to prevent sticking.

Bake for 15 minutes, or until lightly golden. Let cool slightly for 20 to 25 minutes.

Lower the oven temperature to 300°F.

Using a sharp knife, cut each log lengthwise into ½-inch-thick slices. Lay the slices down flat, return to the oven, and bake for another 30 minutes or so until golden. Let cool completely.

Once the cookies are completely cooled, dip half of each cookie in chocolate and roll in almonds. Chill biscotti until the chocolate coating hardens. Store in refrigerator until serving.

ITALIAN WEDDING COOKIES
BISCOTTI DA RICEVIMENTO MATRIMONIALE

MAKES ABOUT 24 COOKIES

These delicate, buttery cookies melt my heart because they melt in my mouth. They are great for weddings, and even better for those days when you fantasize about your someday wedding!

½ cup blanched slivered or sliced almonds

1 cup vegan margarine

1½ cups all-purpose flour*

½ cup powdered sugar, plus extra for dusting

1 teaspoon pure almond or vanilla extract

¼ teaspoon salt

*For a gluten-free alternative, substitute gluten-free all-purpose flour plus ¼ teaspoon xanthan gum and see page 257.

Preheat the oven to 350°F. Line two or three large baking sheets with parchment paper.

In a food processor, pulse almonds until very finely ground. Add margarine, flour, ½ cup powdered sugar, almond extract, and salt and process until the dough comes together, stopping to scrape down the sides. Transfer to a bowl and scoop about 1 rounded tablespoon of dough at a time onto the prepared baking sheets, leaving about 2 inches between each scoop. Bake for 12 to 15 minutes, until lightly golden around the edges. Remove from oven and sift powdered sugar over hot cookies. Let cool and dust with powdered sugar again before serving.

LA BUONA CUCINA RENDE ALLEGRI.

(LAUGHTER IS BRIGHTEST WHERE FOOD IS BEST.)

FLORENTINE BAR COOKIES

BARRETTE ALLA FIORENTINA

MAKES 32 (2-INCH) BARS

This is my mom's secret recipe for chocolate-dipped almond Florentine cookies. While other kids were eating Oreos, my brother and I would get these in our lunch boxes because they were our favorite cookies. Whether in your lunch box or served at a dinner party, these decadent bar cookies are gorgeous and delicious.

Preheat the oven to 350°F. Grease a 9 x 13-inch baking pan well.

For the crust: Place all ingredients in a food processor and pulse about 20 times until it looks like fine meal. Spread the mixture into the prepared pan and press down firmly. Bake for 10 minutes until it is partially baked. It should be just slightly golden and dry to the touch.

For the almond topping: In a medium saucepan, combine margarine, sugar, nondairy milk, and agave. Bring to a boil over medium-high heat, and continue to boil for 10 minutes. Watch the pan carefully and adjust the temperature so that it does not boil over. After 10 minutes, remove pan from heat, add almonds and flour, and stir quickly until combined.

Spread the filling carefully over the partially baked crust and return the pan to the oven and bake for 18 to 20 minutes, until the almonds are golden. The topping will firm up as it cools. Let cool completely before cutting into small squares.

For the chocolate dip: Melt chocolate chips in a double boiler or microwave. Dip or drizzle each bar with melted chocolate.

Refrigerate the bars until chocolate coating has firmed up.

CRUST

½ cup plus 2 tablespoons vegan margarine

½ cup sugar

¼ teaspoon salt

1½ cups all-purpose flour

½ teaspoon pure vanilla extract

ALMOND TOPPING

½ cup vegan margarine

½ cup sugar

½ cup soy, almond, or rice milk

3 tablespoons agave

2 cups sliced almonds

¼ cup all-purpose flour

CHOCOLATE DIP

1 heaping cup semisweet chocolate chips (dairy-free)

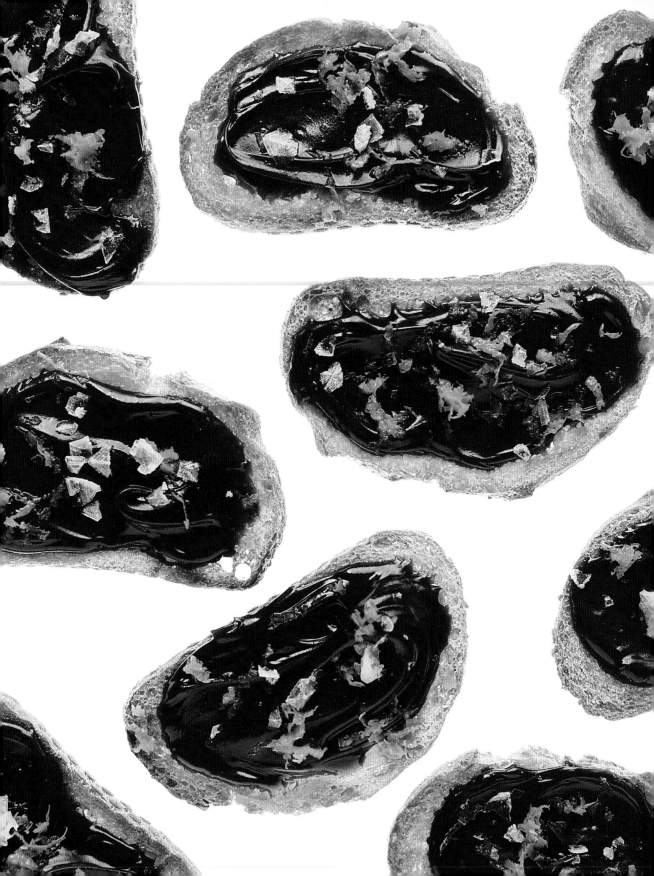

DARK CHOCOLATE CROSTINI WITH SEA SALT AND ORANGE ZEST

CROSTINI DI CIOCCOLATO FONDENTE CON SALE MARINO E SCORZE D'ARANCIA

SERVES 6 TO 8

This is a novel dessert to whip up after dinner if you have some leftover baguette and a bag of chocolate chips in your fridge. It's so easy, but guests always think it's gourmet, too. Kids love it and tend to end up with chocolate all over their faces.

For the crostini: Preheat the oven to 425°F.

Place bread slices on a large baking tray and brush lightly with oil. Bake for 5 to 8 minutes, or until lightly browned on top.

Immediately top each crostini with chocolate pieces, turn off oven, and return to oven for 1 minute, until melted enough to spread. Remove from oven, smooth chocolate with a mini offset spatula or knife. Sprinkle with salt and orange zest.

1 thin baguette, cut into ¼-inch slices on the diagonal

Olive oil for brushing

1 cup chopped dark chocolate or chocolate chips (dairy-free)

Fleur de sel or coarse salt for sprinkling

1 small orange for zesting

OLIVE OIL PANCAKES

FRITTELLE ALL'OLIO DI OLIVA

SERVES 2 TO 3

This recipe is so simple, yet purely divine. Serve with fresh berries and a drizzle of olive oil or maple syrup. You could even add some shards of dark chocolate.

1 cup all-purpose flour*

1 tablespoon baking powder

½ teaspoon salt

¾ cup water

3 tablespoons maple syrup, plus extra for serving

Olive oil

*For a gluten-free alternative, substitute gluten-free all-purpose flour plus ½ teaspoon xanthan gum (page 257).

In a medium bowl, whisk flour, baking powder, and salt. In a separate small bowl or liquid measuring cup, whisk water and maple syrup. Add the liquid to the flour mixture and whisk until just combined. Do not overmix; the batter should have some lumps.

Drizzle a large nonstick skillet or griddle with oil and heat over medium-high heat. For each pancake, pour ¼ cup of batter onto the skillet, and when small bubbles appear in the center of the pancake, it is time to flip it. Let it cook on the other side until lightly browned and cooked through, about 1 minute. Repeat with remaining batter, adding more oil to the skillet as needed. Serve pancakes with warm maple syrup or a drizzle of oil.

MARMALADE PANCAKES
FRITTELLE ALLA MARMELLATA D'ARANCIA

SERVES 2 TO 3

Ribbons of orange marmalade turn these pancakes from ordinary to a breakfast of champions. Don't be alarmed by the large amount of baking powder—you won't be able to taste it, but it binds the pancakes and makes them super light and fluffy!

In a large bowl, whisk flour, baking powder, and salt. In a separate small bowl or measuring cup, whisk water and maple syrup. Add the liquid to the flour mixture and whisk until just combined. Do not overmix; the batter will be thick and should have some lumps. Gently fold in marmalade and chocolate chips.

Lightly oil a large nonstick skillet or griddle and heat over medium-high heat. For each pancake, pour ¼ cup of batter onto the skillet. Adjust heat as needed. When small bubbles appear in the center of the pancake, it is time to flip it. Let it cook on the other side until lightly browned and cooked through, about 1 minute. Repeat with remaining batter, adding more oil to the skillet as needed. If batter gets too thick, add a tablespoon of water as needed. Serve pancakes with dusted powdered sugar and a side of marmalade.

1 cup all-purpose flour*

1 tablespoon baking powder

½ teaspoon salt

¾ cup water

3 tablespoons maple syrup

¼ cup orange marmalade, plus extra for serving

¼ cup semisweet chocolate chips (dairy-free)

Canola oil

Powdered sugar for serving

*For a gluten-free alternative, substitute gluten-free all-purpose flour plus ½ teaspoon xanthan gum (page 257).

ORANGE-ZESTED CHOCOLATE CHIP SCONES
FOCACCINE CON LE SCORZE D'ARANCIA E GOCCE DI CIOCCOLATO

MAKES 8 SCONES

I used to think of scones as those dry-looking stale ones sitting in a bakery counter at your local coffee shop. Yuck! On scone day in culinary school, I knew I had to step it up. These scones are moist and delicate on the inside, with a crisp sugar-sprinkled top. They have a hint of orange zest, a dash of cinnamon, and are dotted with chocolate chips. They are simply irresistible!

2 cups all-purpose flour*, plus extra for work surface

⅓ cup sugar, plus extra for sprinkling

1 tablespoon baking powder

½ teaspoon salt

½ teaspoon ground cinnamon

¼ cup vegan margarine or refined coconut oil

½ cup soy, almond, or rice milk, plus extra for brushing

2 tablespoons freshly squeezed orange juice

Zest of 1 medium orange

⅔ cup semisweet chocolate chips (dairy-free)

*For a gluten-free alternative, substitute gluten-free all-purpose flour plus 1½ teaspoons xanthan gum (page 257).

Preheat the oven to 375°F. Line a large baking sheet with parchment paper.

You can make the dough by hand or use a food processor.

By hand: In a medium bowl, whisk flour, sugar, baking powder, salt, and cinnamon. Cut in margarine using a pastry cutter, until the texture is crumbly. Add nondairy milk, orange juice, zest, and chocolate chips, and mix with a wooden spoon. Do not overmix; the dough should be sticky and wet.

Food processor: In a food processor, process flour, sugar, baking powder, salt, and cinnamon until combined. Add margarine, and pulse until the mixture is crumbly. Add nondairy milk, orange juice, and zest, and pulse until the dough just comes together to form a sticky and wet mixture. Do not overmix. Transfer to a bowl and fold in chocolate chips.

Transfer the dough to a lightly floured surface and liberally flour the top of the dough. Pat the dough into a circle (about 1 inch thick). Using a sharp knife, cut the dough (like you are cutting a pizza) into 8 triangular slices. Transfer each slice to the prepared baking sheet, leaving 2 inches between each slice. Brush the tops with nondairy milk and generously sprinkle with sugar. Bake for about 15 minutes, until just golden on top. Let cool and serve.

CHLOE'S "NUTELLA" CINNAMON ROLLS
GIRELLE DI NUTELLA AROMATIZZATE ALLA CANNELLA

MAKES 12 ROLLS

The title of this one says it all. Homemade almond Nutella-inspired spread laced inside piping hot cinnamon rolls. I can eat about 3½ of these at a time—what about you?

MAKE-AHEAD TIP: After the assembled unbaked cinnamon rolls have risen, cover them in plastic wrap in the pan and refrigerate overnight. Remove plastic wrap and bake the next day, according to recipe directions.

Start this recipe by making Chloe's Vegan "Nutella" (page 247).

For the dough: In a small saucepan, whisk nondairy milk, ½ cup of the sugar, margarine, and salt over low heat until combined. Remove from heat and add vanilla. Let it cool until very warm to the touch, about 110°F.

While the mixture is cooling, place the warm water, remaining 1 tablespoon sugar, and yeast in a 1-cup glass measuring cup. Stir for a second and set aside for about 10 minutes. The yeast will become foamy, double in size, and reach the ¾-cup line. If it does not do so, then the yeast is dead or the water was not at the proper temperature, so make another yeast mixture before proceeding to the next step.

In a stand mixer fitted with a whisk or paddle attachment, combine the nondairy milk mixture and the yeast mixture, and beat at medium speed for about 1 minute. Reduce the speed to low, and add 2½ cups of the flour. Beat until incorporated and add the remaining 2½ cups flour. Beat for about 2 more minutes. Remove the dough from the mixing bowl; it will be somewhat wet and sticky. Place it on a floured surface and knead for about 2 minutes with your hands until the dough is soft and pliable. You can add more flour to keep the dough from sticking to your hands.

DOUGH

1 cup soy, almond, or rice milk

½ cup plus 1 tablespoon sugar

½ cup vegan margarine

½ teaspoon salt

1 teaspoon pure vanilla extract

½ cup warm water, about 110°F

1 packet active dry yeast (2¼ teaspoons)

5 cups all-purpose flour,* plus extra for rolling

Canola oil for greasing

FILLING

½ cup brown sugar

2 teaspoons ground cinnamon

4 tablespoons vegan margarine, melted

Vegan "Nutella" (page 247)

GLAZE

2 cups powdered sugar

4 tablespoons water

*For a gluten-free alternative, substitute gluten-free all-purpose flour plus 2 tablespoons xanthan gum (page 257). If dough seems too dry, add water, 1 tablespoon at a time, until dough is more pliable.

Transfer the dough to a large well-oiled bowl. Cover with a dry kitchen towel and place in a warm part of the kitchen. Let it sit until it has doubled in volume, about 1½ hours (see Tip, below).

Remove the kitchen towel and punch your fist in the center of the dough, so that the dough deflates. Take the dough out and put it on a floured surface, cover with the kitchen towel, and let rest for about 10 minutes.

For the filling and to assemble the rolls: Lightly grease a 9 x 13-inch pan.

Roll the dough out on a lightly floured surface into approximately a 20 x 12-inch rectangle. Combine brown sugar and cinnamon in a small bowl. Brush melted margarine over the entire surface of the dough, then sprinkle the brown sugar mixture evenly over the surface. Place spoonfuls of the vegan nutella over the surface of the dough.

With the long end toward you, roll the dough up evenly. With the seam side down, use a sharp knife to cut the log in half. Then cut each half into 6 equal pieces. You will have 12 cinnamon rolls. Place the rolls, cut side up, into the prepared pan, in 4 rows with 3 rolls in each row, leaving some space between them. Cover with a dry kitchen towel and place in a warm part of the kitchen for the second rise until the rolls have risen and expanded, about 1 hour.

Once the rolls have risen, preheat the oven to 375°F. Bake, uncovered, for 20 to 25 minutes until lightly browned on top. Let the rolls cool for about 10 minutes before glazing.

For the glaze: Combine powdered sugar and water, and whisk until smooth.

Drizzle the glaze over the rolls. Serve warm or at room temperature.

CHLOE'S TIP: RISING DOUGH

If your kitchen is cold, use this trick to create a warm environment for your dough to rise. Heat the oven to 200°F, then turn it off. Let the covered bowl of dough sit in the oven until it doubles in size.

ROSEMARY LEMON SHORTBREAD COOKIES
FROLLINI AL LIMONE E ROSMARINO

MAKES 25 SMALL SQUARES

Delicate, buttery shortbread with a hint of rosemary and lemon zest. There's no reason not to eat this at breakfast, lunch, and dinner.

Preheat the oven to 350°F. Lightly grease an 8-inch square pan and line with parchment paper long enough to overhang the edges.

In a food processor, pulse flour, sugar, salt, rosemary, and zest until combined. Add margarine and pulse until crumbly and incorporated. Press the dough firmly into the prepared pan and pat the top until smooth. Bake for 20 to 22 minutes, until very lightly browned around the edges. Let cool in the pan.

Once cooled, lift the parchment paper to release the cookies from the pan and unmold. Using a sharp knife, cut into 25 squares.

1¾ cups all-purpose flour*

½ cup powdered sugar

¼ teaspoon salt

1 tablespoon chopped fresh rosemary leaves

4 tablespoons lemon zest (about 4 lemons)

¾ cup vegan margarine

*For a gluten-free alternative, substitute gluten-free all-purpose flour plus ¼ teaspoon xanthan gum (page 257).

CHOCOLATE CHERRY COFFEE CAKE*
TORTA AL CAFFÈ CON CIOCCOLATO E CILIEGIE

SERVES 6 TO 8

This coffee cake is very moist with a crunchy crumb topping that melts in your mouth. This one isn't just for breakfast or brunch; I often serve it as a dinner party dessert, too! Don't be alarmed by the extra-thick crumb topping—that's what makes for an extraordinary coffee cake.

MAKE-AHEAD TIP: Cake batter and streusel topping can be assembled in the pan, covered with plastic wrap, and refrigerated overnight. Bake fresh the next morning.

For the topping: In a medium bowl, combine flour, sugar, brown sugar, cinnamon, and salt. Add margarine and toss with two forks, as though you were tossing a salad, until it appears crumbly. The crumbs should be lumpy, about the size of peas.

For the cake: Preheat the oven to 350°F. Lightly grease a 9-inch round or square cake pan.

In a large bowl, whisk flour, sugar, brown sugar, baking soda, baking powder, and salt. In another bowl, whisk non-dairy milk, oil, vinegar, and almond extract. Pour the wet mixture into the dry mixture and whisk until just combined. Do not overmix. Gently fold in cherries and chocolate chips.

Spread the batter into the prepared pan and sprinkle with the topping, scrunching some of the topping together to integrate some larger lumps. Bake for 45 to 50 minutes, or until a toothpick inserted in the center comes out dry with a few crumbs clinging to it. Let cool and slice. Dust with powdered sugar before serving.

TOPPING

1¼ cups all-purpose flour*

⅓ cup sugar

⅓ cup brown sugar

2 teaspoons ground cinnamon

¼ teaspoon salt

½ cup vegan margarine, melted

CAKE

1 cup all-purpose flour*

¼ cup sugar

¼ cup brown sugar

½ teaspoon baking soda

½ teaspoon baking powder

¼ teaspoon salt

½ cup soy, almond, or rice milk

¼ cup canola oil

2 teaspoons white or apple cider vinegar

1 teaspoon pure almond extract

1 cup cherries, fresh or frozen

½ cup semisweet chocolate chips (dairy-free)

Powdered sugar for serving

*For a gluten-free cake, substitute gluten-free all-purpose flour plus ½ teaspoon xanthan gum (page 257). For a gluten-free topping, substitute gluten-free all-purpose flour plus ½ teaspoon xanthan gum.

CHOCOLATE CHIP ZUCCHINI MUFFINS
MUFFINS DI ZUCCHINE CON GOCCE DI CIOCCOLATO

MAKES ABOUT 16 MUFFINS

These perfect little muffins are great served at any time of day. The zucchini adds extreme moistness and richness to the chocolate, so it's a great way to sneak in some veggies for the kids—or the adults.

MAKE-AHEAD TIP: Muffins can be made in advance and frozen for up to 1 month. Thaw muffins and dust with powdered sugar before serving.

Preheat the oven to 350°F. Line two 12-cup cupcake pans with 16 cupcake liners.

In a large bowl, whisk flour, sugar, cocoa, baking soda, and salt. In a separate bowl, whisk water, oil, vinegar, and vanilla. Pour the wet mixture into the dry mixture and whisk until just combined. Do not overmix. Fold in zucchini and chocolate chips.

Fill the cupcake liners about two-thirds full with batter. Bake for about 20 minutes, or until a toothpick inserted in the center of the muffin comes out dry, with a few crumbs clinging to it. Let the muffins cool completely.

Dust the muffins with powdered sugar and serve.

1½ cups all-purpose flour*

1 cup sugar

⅓ cup unsweetened cocoa powder

1 teaspoon baking soda

½ teaspoon salt

¾ cup water

½ cup canola oil

2 tablespoons white or apple-cider vinegar

1 tablespoon pure vanilla extract

1½ cups shredded zucchini, about 2, squeezed dry with a paper towel (see Tip below)

½ cup semisweet chocolate chips (dairy-free)

Powdered sugar for serving

*For a gluten-free alternative, substitute gluten-free all-purpose flour plus ¾ teaspoon xanthan gum (page 257).

CHLOE'S TIP:

Cut zucchini in half crosswise and grate the circular cut sides. That way you will get short grated strips.

BANANA COFFEE CUPCAKES *
PASTICCINI DI CAFFÈ E BANANA

MAKES 18 CUPCAKES

I made these cupcakes with my culinary interns and they went crazy for them. Some said they were the best cupcakes they've ever had, vegan or not! The banana cupcake is moist, dotted with chocolate chips, and subtly spiced—perfect with a blanket of silky cappuccino frosting.

MAKE-AHEAD TIP: Cupcakes can be made in advance and frozen, unfrosted, for up to 1 month. Thaw cupcakes and frost before serving.

For the cupcakes: Preheat the oven to 350°F. Line two 12-cup cupcake pans with 18 cupcake liners.

In a large bowl, whisk flour, sugar, baking powder, baking soda, salt, cinnamon, nutmeg, cloves, and ginger. In a separate bowl, whisk bananas, coconut milk, oil, vinegar, and vanilla. Pour the wet mixture into the dry mixture and whisk until just combined. Do not overmix. Gently fold in chocolate chips.

Fill the cupcake liners about two-thirds full with batter. Bake for 18 to 20 minutes, or until a toothpick inserted in the center of the cupcake comes out clean with a few crumbs clinging to it. Cool the cupcakes completely before frosting.

For the frosting: Using a handheld or stand mixer, beat the shortening until smooth. With the mixer running on low, add powdered sugar and vanilla, and beat to incorporate. Add 1 tablespoon of espresso liquid at a time, as needed, until it reaches desired frosting consistency and espresso flavor. You may not need to use all of the espresso liquid. Beat on high for 2 minutes, until light and fluffy.

To assemble the cupcakes: Spread a layer of frosting over each cupcake.

BANANA CUPCAKES

2 cups all-purpose flour*

1 cup sugar

1 teaspoon baking powder

½ teaspoon baking soda

1 teaspoon salt

½ teaspoon ground cinnamon

½ teaspoon ground nutmeg

½ teaspoon ground cloves

½ teaspoon ground ginger

1 cup mashed bananas (about 2 very ripe bananas)

1 cup canned coconut milk, mixed well before measuring

½ cup canola oil

1 tablespoon white or apple cider vinegar

1 tablespoon pure vanilla extract

1½ cups semisweet chocolate chips (dairy-free)

COFFEE FROSTING

1 cup nonhydrogenated vegetable shortening

3 cups powdered sugar

1 teaspoon pure vanilla extract

2 tablespoons instant espresso powder dissolved in 2 tablespoons water

*For a gluten-free alternative, substitute gluten-free all-purpose flour plus 1 teaspoon xanthan gum (page 257).

LEMON THYME CUPCAKES
PASTICCINI DI LIMONE E TIMO

MAKES ABOUT 15 CUPCAKES

These cupcakes are light and fluffy with a subtle citrus-herb flavor. For anyone who's "not a dessert person," these cupcakes will slyly pull them to the other side.

NOTE: Frosted cupcakes should be stored in the refrigerator until serving.

For the cupcakes: Preheat the oven to 350°F. Line two 12-cup cupcake pans with 15 cupcake liners. Lightly grease the liners with baking spray.

In a large bowl, whisk flour, baking soda, baking powder, and salt. In a separate bowl, whisk oil, maple syrup, water, lemon juice and zest, lemon extract, and thyme. Pour the wet mixture into the dry mixture and whisk until just combined. Do not overmix.

Fill the cupcake liners about two-thirds full with batter. Bake for 16 to 17 minutes, or until a toothpick inserted in the center of the cupcake comes out dry with a few crumbs clinging to it. Let the cupcakes cool completely before frosting.

To assemble the cupcakes: Dust the cooled cupcakes with powdered sugar and pipe or spoon a dollop of coconut whipped cream on the cupcakes. Garnish with thyme and lemon zest. Store in refrigerator until serving.

2 cups all-purpose flour*

1 teaspoon baking soda

1 teaspoon baking powder

½ teaspoon salt

½ cup canola oil

¾ cup maple syrup

¾ cup water

¼ cup lemon juice

2 tablespoons lemon zest, plus extra for garnish (about 3 lemons)

1 tablespoon pure lemon extract

2 tablespoons fresh thyme leaves, plus extra for garnish

Powdered sugar for serving

Coconut Whipped Cream (page 245)

*For a gluten-free alternative, substitute gluten-free all-purpose flour plus 1 teaspoon xanthan gum (page 257).

RASPBERRY TIRAMISU CUPCAKES
PASTICCINI AL TIRAMISÙ CON LAMPONI

MAKES 14 CUPCAKES

This cupcake took first prize on Food Network's Cupcake Wars and stood its ground against four other contestants' nonvegan cupcakes! It is an espresso- and amaretto-soaked cupcake, filled with coffee crème, ground chocolate, and fresh raspberry puree.

For the cupcakes: Preheat the oven to 350°F. Line two 12-cup cupcake pans with 14 cupcake liners.

In a large bowl, whisk flour, sugar, baking soda, baking powder, and salt. In a separate bowl, whisk nondairy milk, oil, vinegar, and vanilla. Pour the wet mixture into the dry mixture and whisk until just combined. Do not overmix.

Fill the cupcake liners about two-thirds full. Bake for 16 to 18 minutes, or until a toothpick inserted in the center of the cupcake comes out dry. Let the cupcakes cool completely.

For the espresso soak: In a small bowl, whisk amaretto and espresso powder until espresso dissolves. Set aside.

For the raspberry sauce: In a medium saucepan, cook raspberries, water, sugar, and salt over medium heat for about 15 minutes, or until thick and saucy. Remove from heat and stir in lemon juice. Let cool, then store in refrigerator.

For the frosting: Using a mixer, slowly beat the shortening, powdered sugar, vanilla, and 1 tablespoon espresso-amaretto liquid at a time, as needed, until desired consistency. Beat on high for 2 minutes, until light and fluffy.

To assemble the cupcakes: Using a spoon, cut out a small hole from the top of each cupcake. In the hole of the cupcake, drizzle the espresso soak, raspberry sauce, 2 teaspoons of ground chocolate, if using, and piped frosting on top. Garnish with a raspberry and mint leaf, if using.

VANILLA CUPCAKES

1½ cups all-purpose flour

¾ cup sugar

½ teaspoon baking soda

½ teaspoon baking powder

½ teaspoon salt

¾ cup soy, almond, or rice milk

½ cup canola oil

2 tablespoons white or apple cider vinegar

2 teaspoons pure vanilla extract

ESPRESSO SOAK

⅓ cup amaretto

1 tablespoon instant espresso powder

RASPBERRY SAUCE

1 (12-ounce) bag frozen raspberries or 2 cups fresh

2 tablespoons water

¼ cup sugar

⅛ teaspoon salt

1 teaspoon lemon juice

FROSTING

1 cup nonhydrogenated vegetable shortening

3 cups powdered sugar

1 teaspoon pure vanilla extract

2 tablespoons instant espresso powder dissolved in 2 tablespoons amaretto

GARNISH (OPTIONAL)

½ cup ground semisweet chocolate (dairy-free)

Fresh raspberries

Small mint leaves

CHOCOLATE ALMOND MOUSSE CAKE
MOUSSE DI CIOCCOLATO E MANDORLE

MAKES TWO 9-INCH ROUND LAYERS

This is a big, impressive showstopper. It has several steps, but the result is worth it. Everyone in my family demands it on birthdays . . . and on ordinary days, too. The chocolate cake is always moist and the mousse is light and fluffy. You will certainly be a hit at the next party if you come with this as your plus one.

NOTE: Mousse filling will need to chill overnight in the refrigerator.

MAKE-AHEAD TIP: Cake layers can be made in advance and frozen, unfrosted, for up to 1 month. Thaw cakes and frost before serving.

For the mousse filling: Chill the bowl and whisk of a stand mixer in the freezer for about 15 minutes. If they are not very cold, the mousse will not whip properly.

In the meantime, whisk nondairy milk and espresso powder, if using, in a medium saucepan over medium heat. Once espresso is incorporated, add chocolate chips and whisk over low heat until the chocolate is melted and smooth. Pour the mixture into a large bowl, let cool, then chill in the refrigerator, stirring often, until cool to the touch, about 15 minutes. Watch carefully—if chocolate chills for too long, it might be hard to beat.

Skim the solidified coconut cream from the chilled can of coconut milk and transfer the solids to the chilled bowl of the stand mixer. Do not include any of the coconut water, even if you have to leave behind a little margin of coconut cream (a little bit of coconut water can harm your results).

Add powdered sugar and beat on high speed for 1 to 2 minutes, until fluffy. Add the cooled chocolate mixture and beat until incorporated. Let chill, covered, in the refrigerator overnight.

MOUSSE FILLING

½ cup soy, almond, or rice milk

1 teaspoon instant espresso powder, optional

1 cup semisweet chocolate chips (dairy-free)

1 (13.5-ounce) can coconut milk (not light), preferably Thai Kitchen or Whole Foods 365, chilled in the refrigerator overnight (be sure not to shake or stir)

¼ cup powdered sugar

CAKE

2 cups all-purpose flour*

2 cups sugar

1 cup finely ground blanched almonds or almond meal

½ cup unsweetened cocoa powder

2 teaspoons baking soda

1 teaspoon salt

2 cups water

1 cup canola oil

¼ cup white or apple cider vinegar

1 tablespoon pure vanilla extract

1 tablespoon instant espresso powder

Powdered sugar or Chocolate Ganache (page 245) for topping

*For a gluten-free alternative, substitute gluten-free all-purpose flour plus 1 teaspoon xanthan gum (page 257).

For the cake: Preheat the oven to 350°F. Lightly grease two 9-inch round cake pans and line the bottoms with parchment paper.

In a large bowl, whisk flour, sugar, ground almonds, cocoa, baking soda, and salt. In a separate bowl, whisk water, oil, vinegar, vanilla, and espresso. Pour the wet mixture into the dry mixture and whisk until just combined. Do not overmix.

Fill the prepared cake pans evenly with batter. Bake for about 35 minutes, or until a toothpick inserted in the center of the cake comes out dry with a few crumbs clinging to it. Rotate the cake halfway through baking time. Let the cakes cool completely before assembly.

To assemble the cake: Once the cakes are completely cooled, run a knife around the inside edge of each cake pan to loosen, and gently unmold the cake. Peel off the parchment paper. Place one cake on a serving plate or cardboard cake circle. Spread the mousse filling on top of the cake. Place the second cake on top of the first. Store in refrigerator until serving. Dust the top with powdered sugar or top with chocolate ganache and serve.

POMEGRANATE MINT ITALIAN SODA
BEVANDA GASSATA ALLA MENTA E MELOGRANO

SERVES 6 TO 8

Don't be fooled by the fancy-sounding title: This agave-sweetened beverage can hold its own among kids too! My recipe tester Ann Marie served it to her three-year-old son, Matthew. He said it was "his favorite drink ever" and asked her to make it again for him the next day. Kids are always very honest, so you can trust that this one is a winner.

In a large pitcher, combine seltzer, pomegranate juice, agave, and lime juice. Chill and serve over ice with a sprig of fresh mint in each glass.

1 liter seltzer water

2 cups pure pomegranate juice

½ cup agave

¼ cup lime juice

8 sprigs fresh mint

LEMON THYME ITALIAN SODA
BEVANDA GASSATA AL LIMONE E TIMO

SERVES 6 TO 8

The combination of lemon and thyme is so refreshing, which makes this a perfect beverage to serve with a hearty Italian meal. For the adults, add a splash of vodka to each serving. Be careful—the soda flavor masks the alcohol!

MAKE-AHEAD TIP: Lemon Thyme syrup can be made in advance and stored in the refrigerator for up to 2 days.

In a medium saucepan, combine thyme, sugar, and water. Bring to a boil, and then reduce heat and let simmer for 5 minutes, stirring frequently. Remove from heat, strain liquid into a pitcher, and discard thyme. Let cool completely. Stir in lemon juice and seltzer. Taste, and add more seltzer if needed. Chill and serve over ice with a sprig of thyme for garnish.

½ bunch fresh thyme sprigs (about ½ ounce), plus extra for garnish

1 cup sugar

1 cup water

1½ cups lemon juice

1 liter seltzer water, plus extra if needed

STRAWBERRY BASIL MILKSHAKE*
FRAPPÈ CON FRAGOLE E BASILICO

SERVES 3

Peace, love, and vegan milkshakes! You'd be surprised how complementary the basil is to the strawberries and cream. Superb. You'll probably want to eat this one with a spoon (like me!) or at least use an extra-thick straw.

1 cup soy, almond, or rice milk, plus extra if needed

1 pint dairy-free vanilla ice cream

2 cups frozen strawberries

2 tablespoons agave

½ cup fresh basil leaves (about 12 leaves)

In a blender, combine all ingredients except basil and blend until smooth. Add more nondairy milk if needed. Add basil and blend until just incorporated.

ITALIAN WEDDING CAKE
TORTA NUZIALE

MAKES TWO 9-INCH ROUND LAYERS

This cake is so delicious that if you want a shortcut you can skip the frosting and simply dust the tops with powdered sugar. The cake is the easy part—now I just need to find someone to marry! Any takers?

MAKE-AHEAD TIP: Cake layers can be made in advance and frozen, unfrosted, for up to 1 month. Thaw and frost before serving.

For the cake: Preheat the oven to 350°F. Lightly grease two 9-inch round cake pans and line the bottoms with parchment paper.

In a large bowl, whisk flour, sugar, baking soda, and salt. In a separate bowl, whisk nondairy milk, oil, vinegar, vanilla, and almond extract. Pour the wet mixture into the dry mixture and whisk until just combined. Do not overmix. Gently fold in coconut, pecans, and pineapple.

Fill each prepared cake pan evenly with batter. Bake for 35 to 40 minutes, or until a toothpick inserted in the center of the cake comes out dry, with a few crumbs clinging to it. Rotate the cakes halfway through baking time. Let the cakes cool completely before assembly.

To assemble the cake: Once the cakes have completely cooled, run a knife around the inside edge of each cake pan to loosen, and gently unmold. Peel off the parchment paper. Place one cake on a serving plate or cardboard cake circle, and slide strips of parchment paper under the edges of the bottom of the cake to prevent frosting from getting on the plate. Spread a thin layer of frosting on top of the cake. Place the second cake on top of the first and spread a thin layer of frosting on top. Frost sides, if desired. Garnish with edible flowers, if desired.

3 cups all-purpose flour*

2 cups sugar

2 teaspoons baking soda

1 teaspoon salt

2 cups soy, almond, or rice milk

1 cup canola oil

¼ cup white or apple cider vinegar

1 tablespoon pure vanilla extract

1 teaspoon pure almond extract

1 cup shredded coconut (sweetened or unsweetened)

1 cup chopped pecans

1 (8-ounce) can crushed pineapple, undrained

Frosting (page 214)

Edible flowers for garnish (optional), see Tip (page 214)

*For a gluten-free alternative, substitute gluten-free all-purpose flour plus 1½ teaspoons xanthan gum (page 257).

FROSTING

1 cup nonhydrogenated vegetable shortening

3 cups powdered sugar

1 teaspoon pure vanilla extract

3 to 5 tablespoons soy, almond, or rice milk

1 cup chopped pecans

Using a stand or hand mixer, beat shortening until smooth. With the mixer running on low, add powdered sugar, vanilla, and 1 tablespoon nondairy milk at a time, as needed, until frosting reaches a spreadable consistency. Increase the speed to high and beat for 2 minutes, until light and fluffy. Beat in pecans.

CHLOE'S TIP: EDIBLE FLOWERS

I love purchasing edible flowers at my local gourmet grocery store or farmers' market. It's the easiest and most elegant way to top a cake for an event. When I worked at Millennium Restaurant in San Francisco, we topped our wedding cakes exclusively with the finest flowers.

VANILLA GELATO
GELATO ALLA VANIGLIA

SERVES 6

In a blender, combine all ingredients. Blend until smooth. Chill in the refrigerator for 3 hours. Once the ice cream base is chilled, prepare in an ice cream maker according to manufacturer's instructions. Store in freezer with plastic wrap pressed tightly against the surface.

1 (13.5 ounce) can coconut milk

½ cup agave or maple syrup

1 tablespoon canola oil

¼ teaspoon guar gum (page 257)

Seeds scraped from 1 vanilla bean

1 teaspoon pure vanilla extract

1 teaspoon bourbon

Pinch of salt

AFFOGATO (VANILLA GELATO DROWNED IN A SHOT OF ESPRESSO)
AFFOGATO DI GELATO ALLA VANIGLIA

SERVES 4

Affogato is a traditional Italian dessert that means vanilla gelato drowned in a shot of espresso. If you have kids at the dinner table, replace the espresso with soy or almond milk hot cocoa (you can find a recipe for my absolute favorite hot cocoa in Chloe's Vegan Desserts).

Serve a few scoops of ice cream in each bowl and top with a shot (or about ¼ cup) of hot espresso. Serve immediately.

1 recipe Vanilla Gelato (above) or 1 pint dairy-free vanilla ice cream

1 cup hot brewed espresso

ROASTED BANANA BOURBON ICE CREAM
GELATO AL BOURBON CON BANANA ARROSTITA

MAKES 1 PINT

To make this ice cream, I blend caramelized roasted bananas with coconut milk and a touch of bourbon. Yum! If you're bananas for bananas, roast some extra bananas to chop and place on top. And if you're more of a chocolate lover, drape it with a layer of Hot Fudge (page 227).

3 medium bananas, peeled and cut into ½-inch slices

1 tablespoon canola oil, plus extra for brushing

1 (13.5-ounce) can coconut milk

⅓ cup agave or maple syrup

1 teaspoon pure vanilla extract

2 tablespoons bourbon

¼ teaspoon salt

Preheat the oven to 400°F.

Lightly brush banana slices with oil on all sides and arrange on a large baking sheet. Roast for 30 minutes. Remove from oven and let cool.

In a blender combine roasted bananas, oil, coconut milk, agave, vanilla, bourbon, and salt. Blend until completely smooth and no chunks of banana remain. Chill in the refrigerator for 3 hours. Once the ice cream base is chilled, prepare in an ice cream maker according to manufacturer's instructions. Store in freezer with plastic wrap pressed tightly against the surface.

CHLOE'S TIP: ICE CREAM

When making an ice cream base, it should taste overly sweet and salty. Once it is frozen and churned into ice cream, the cold temperature mutes the flavor somewhat. So if it is too sweet and salty as a base, it will probably taste just right once frozen.

TIRAMISU*

TIRAMISÙ

SERVES 8

In Italian, tiramisù *means "pick me up," because Italian women used to dip leftover biscuits in espresso during the middle of the day for a zing of energy.*

NOTE: Tiramisu will be best if chilled in the refrigerator overnight before serving.

For the cake: Preheat the oven to 350°F. Lightly grease one 9-inch round cake pan.

In a large bowl, whisk flour, sugar, baking soda, and salt. In a separate bowl, whisk water, oil, vinegar, and almond extract. Pour the wet mixture into the dry mixture and whisk until just combined. Do not overmix.

Fill the prepared cake pan with batter. Bake for 28 to 30 minutes, or until a toothpick inserted in the center of the cake comes out dry with a few crumbs clinging to it. Rotate the cake halfway through baking time. Let the cake cool completely before assembly.

For the espresso soak: In a small bowl, whisk water, rum, and espresso powder until espresso dissolves.

To assemble: Cut the cake into 1-inch cubes by scoring with a knife while still in the pan. In a large bowl or trifle bowl, add half of the cake cubes. Evenly drizzle half of the soaking liquid over the cake cubes. Top with dollops of half of the whipped cream and sprinkle with ground chocolate. Repeat layers and chill overnight before serving.

VANILLA CAKE

1½ cups all-purpose flour*

1 cup sugar

1 teaspoon baking soda

½ teaspoon salt

¾ cup water

½ cup canola oil

2 tablespoons white or apple cider vinegar

1 tablespoon pure almond extract

ESPRESSO SOAK

¾ cup water

2 tablespoons dark rum

3 tablespoons instant espresso powder

3 cups Coconut Whipped Cream (page 245)

1 heaping cup semisweet chocolate chips (dairy-free), ground in a food processor or finely chopped

*For a gluten-free alternative, substitute gluten-free all-purpose flour plus ¾ teaspoon xanthan gum (page 257).

ITALIAN APPLE CAKE *

TORTA DI MELA

SERVES 8

You know how every family or household has "the cake"? Well, this is the cake in my New York City apartment. In advance of any birthday or snowy day, my roommates will ask, "Are you making the cake?" We're all obsessed with it. Everyone has her own copy of the recipe and makes it frequently. I have no doubt that if you try this cake once, it will become the cake in your house, too. If you're feeling adventurous, try replacing one of the apples with a pear!

1½ cups all-purpose flour*

¾ cup sugar

¾ teaspoon baking soda

1 teaspoon ground cinnamon

¼ teaspoon salt

½ cup canola oil

¼ cup water

2 teaspoons pure vanilla extract

1 tablespoon white or apple cider vinegar

3 apples, peeled and thinly sliced

Powdered sugar for serving

*For a gluten-free alternative, substitute gluten-free all-purpose flour plus ¾ teaspoon xanthan gum (page 257).

Preheat the oven to 350°F. Lightly grease a 9-inch round pan and line with parchment paper. Grease again.

In a large bowl, whisk flour, sugar, baking soda, cinnamon, and salt. In a separate bowl, whisk oil, water, vanilla, and vinegar. Pour wet ingredients into the dry ingredients and mix with a large spoon until just combined. Do not overmix. Batter will be very thick, but the apples will release moisture as they bake.

Arrange some of the apples in a circular pattern to cover most of the bottom of the prepared cake pan. Then gently fold in the remaining apples into the batter. Spoon the batter into the pan, being careful not to disrupt the apple pattern on the bottom. Use a spatula or your fingertips to pat it evenly into the pan.

Bake for 40 to 45 minutes, or until the center is set and the cake is lightly browned on top. Rotate the cake halfway through baking time.

Once cooled, run a knife around the edges to loosen the cake, and gently unmold so that the apple design is on top. Peel off the parchment paper. Dust with powdered sugar and serve.

LEFTOVER RED WINE CHOCOLATE CAKE WITH DRUNKEN RASPBERRIES

TORTA DI CIOCCOLATO AL VINO ROSSO CON LAMPONI "UBRIACHI"

MAKES ONE 9-INCH ROUND LAYER

Didn't quite finish that bottle of red wine last night? Use it to make chocolate cake! This rich and seductive chocolate cake is fudgy on the inside with a hint of red wine. Top it with wine-soaked "drunken" raspberries and a dollop of coconut whipped cream for the ultimate lovers' dessert.

MAKE-AHEAD TIP: Cake layers can be made in advance and frozen for up to 1 month. Thaw cakes before serving.

CAKE

1½ cups all-purpose flour*

1 cup sugar

⅓ cup unsweetened cocoa powder

1 teaspoon baking soda

½ teaspoon salt

¾ cup dry red wine

½ cup water

½ cup canola oil

2 tablespoons white or apple cider vinegar

1 teaspoon pure vanilla extract

TOPPING

½ cup dry red wine

½ cup sugar

1 small container raspberries (6 ounces)

Powdered sugar for serving

Coconut Whipped Cream (page 245)

*For a gluten-free alternative, substitute gluten-free all-purpose flour plus ¾ teaspoon xanthan gum (page 257).

For the cake: Preheat the oven to 350°F. Lightly grease a 9-inch round cake pan and line the bottom with parchment paper.

In a large bowl, whisk flour, sugar, cocoa, baking soda, and salt. In a separate bowl, whisk wine, water, oil, vinegar, and vanilla. Pour the wet mixture into the dry mixture and whisk until just combined. Do not overmix.

Fill the prepared cake pan with batter. Bake for 28 to 30 minutes, or until a toothpick inserted in the center of the cake comes out dry with a few crumbs clinging to it. Be sure to rotate the cake halfway through baking time. Let the cake cool completely.

For the topping: In a small saucepan, combine wine and sugar and cook over medium heat until sugar dissolves and mixture begins to boil. Let boil for 1 to 2 minutes and remove from heat. Place raspberries in a bowl and pour the wine mixture over the raspberries. Refrigerate and let soak for at least 30 minutes and up to 2 days.

Slice cake and dust each serving with powdered sugar. Then, top each slice with a dollop of whipped cream and spoonful of wine-soaked raspberries.

MINT CHIP GELATO SANDWICHES*
BISCOTTI DI GELATO ALLA MENTA CON GOCCE DI CIOCCOLATO

MAKES ABOUT 10 TO 12 SANDWICHES

I make these ice cream sandwiches for almost every party I host. The mint chip gelato is super creamy (not icy!) and the homemade cookies make these better than any store-bought ice cream sandwich. If you're serving a large crowd, you can make them into minis too. Any leftover cookie dough can be scooped and frozen for another day.

NOTE: Ice cream sandwiches are best if assembled and frozen for at least 24 hours. Ice cream and cookies can also be separately made in advance and frozen.

For the mint chip gelato: Blend coconut milk, agave, oil, guar gum, peppermint, salt, and food coloring in a blender. Chill in the refrigerator for 2 to 3 hours.

Once the ice cream base is chilled, run it in an ice cream maker according to machine instructions. Fold the chocolate chips into the ice cream. Cover bowl with plastic wrap, making sure that the wrap is pressed onto the top of the ice cream. Chill in freezer until firm enough to scoop.

For the chocolate chip cookies: Preheat the oven to 325°F and line a large baking sheet with parchment paper.

In a medium bowl, whisk flour, baking soda, cornstarch, and salt. Using an electric mixer, beat the margarine, sugar, brown sugar, water, and vanilla until fluffy. Stir in the flour mixture, ½ cup at a time, and then add chocolate chips.

Scoop about 2 tablespoons of dough at a time onto the prepared baking sheet and flatten it with the palm of your hand. If dough is too soft, chill in the refrigerator until it is easy to scoop. Repeat with remaining dough, leaving about 2 inches between each cookie. Bake for 15 to 20 minutes, until the edges begin to brown and the center of the cookie is a nice golden color. Rotate the baking sheet halfway through baking time. Remove from oven and let cool completely.

To assemble the ice cream sandwiches: Let the ice cream soften in the refrigerator for 12 to 15 minutes. Place 1 scoop of ice cream between 2 cookies, gently squeeze together, and freeze. Repeat with all remaining cookies. Store in freezer in a single layer (not stacked) for a few hours or overnight until firm.

MINT CHIP GELATO (OR USE STORE-BOUGHT VEGAN MINT CHIP ICE CREAM)

1 (13.5 ounce) can coconut milk

½ cup agave

1 tablespoon canola oil

¼ teaspoon guar gum (page 257)

1 teaspoon pure peppermint extract

Pinch of salt

2 drops green food coloring

½ cup mini chocolate chips (dairy-free)

CHOCOLATE CHIP COOKIES

2¼ cups all-purpose flour*

1 teaspoon baking soda

1 tablespoon cornstarch

1 teaspoon salt

1 cup chilled vegan margarine

¾ cup sugar

¾ cup brown sugar

4 tablespoons water

1 tablespoon pure vanilla extract

1 cup semisweet chocolate chips (dairy-free)

*For a gluten-free alternative, substitute gluten-free all-purpose flour plus ½ teaspoon xanthan gum (page 257).

ESPRESSO CHIP SUNDAES
GELATO ALL'ESPRESSO CON GOCCE DI CIOCCOLATO

SERVES 4 TO 6

My favorite ice cream flavor is definitely coffee. There's nothing like that rich aroma and heavenly flavor. This Espresso Gelato is the ultimate version of coffee ice cream because the texture is so rich and creamy. Top it with all the fixin's of a hot fudge sundae. For a shortcut, use store-bought coffee ice cream (non-dairy).

For the espresso gelato: Blend coconut milk, espresso powder, agave, oil, hazelnut liquor, guar gum, and salt in a blender. Chill in the refrigerator for 2 to 3 hours.

Once the ice cream base is chilled, run it in an ice cream maker according to machine instructions. Fold the desired amount of mini chocolate chips into the ice cream. Cover bowl with plastic wrap, making sure that the wrap is pressed onto the top of the ice cream. Store in freezer.

To assemble the sundaes: Assemble each sundae by scooping the espresso gelato into individual bowls. Top with hot fudge, coconut whipped cream, if using, and toasted almonds.

ESPRESSO GELATO

1 (15-ounce) can coconut milk

2 tablespoons instant espresso powder

½ cup agave or maple syrup

1 tablespoon canola oil

2 teaspoons hazelnut or coffee liquor

¼ teaspoon guar gum (page 257)

Pinch of salt

½ cup mini semisweet chocolate chips (dairy-free)

Hot Fudge (recipe below)

Coconut Whipped Cream (page 245), optional

Toasted chopped or sliced almonds for serving

HOT FUDGE

In a small saucepan, heat coconut milk over medium-high heat until it just boils. Turn heat to low and whisk in chocolate chips. Let cook, whisking frequently, until smooth. Remove from heat and whisk in agave and vanilla.

½ cup canned coconut milk, mixed well before measuring

1 cup semisweet chocolate chips (dairy-free)

1 tablespoon agave or maple syrup

½ teaspoon pure vanilla extract

POLENTA BERRY COBBLER WITH VANILLA GELATO *
CROSTATA DI POLENTA CON MIRTILLI E GELATO ALLA VANIGLIA

MAKES ONE 8-INCH PAN OR 4 RAMEKINS

That's right, you can make cobbler out of our favorite ol' Italian grain, polenta. The polenta gives the sugary biscuit topping a nice crunch and golden hue. What a fantastic break from your everyday cobbler or crisp.

NOTE: For a shortcut, serve with a scoop of store-bought vanilla ice cream (dairy-free).

MAKE-AHEAD TIP: Unbaked cobbler can be assembled and refrigerated overnight. Sprinkle the top with sugar and bake before serving.

FILLING

16 ounces frozen berries
(mixed, blueberries, or cherries)

¼ cup all-purpose flour*

⅓ cup sugar

POLENTA TOPPING

¼ cup medium grind polenta
(not quick-cooking)

1 teaspoon baking powder

¼ teaspoon salt

¾ cup all-purpose flour*

2 tablespoons sugar, plus extra
for sprinkling

3 tablespoons vegan
margarine, melted

½ cup soy, almond, or rice milk

Vanilla Gelato (page 215) or
Coconut Whipped Cream
(page 245) for serving

*For a gluten-free polenta topping,
substitute gluten-free all-purpose
flour plus ½ teaspoon xanthan gum
(page 257). For a gluten-free filling,
substitute gluten-free all-purpose
flour plus ¼ teaspoon xanthan gum.

Preheat the oven to 350°F. Lightly grease an 8-inch square pan.

For the filling: In a large bowl combine all ingredients and place in a prepared pan.

For the polenta topping: In a large bowl, whisk polenta, baking powder, salt, flour, and sugar. Add melted margarine and soy milk, and whisk until combined. Do not overmix. Spoon the batter over the berries; do not worry if it does not cover all the fruit.

Generously sprinkle sugar evenly over the top of the pan. Bake for 40 to 45 minutes, or until polenta is golden and mixture is bubbling around the edges. Remove from the oven and let sit for about 15 minutes. Serve with vanilla gelato or coconut whipped cream.

MAKE-YOUR-OWN BASICS

DOUGH, SAUCES, AND VEGAN CHEESE

ARRABBIATA SAUCE

SUGO ALL'ARRABBIATA

MAKES ABOUT 3½ CUPS

Sure, a store-bought jar of Arrabbiata sauce will do just fine, but if you have the time, why not make your own?

2 tablespoons olive oil

4 garlic cloves, minced

2 teaspoons Italian seasoning

½ teaspoon crushed red pepper

½ teaspoon sea salt

½ teaspoon freshly ground black pepper

1 (28-ounce) can crushed tomatoes

¼ cup soy, almond, or rice milk

1 tablespoon brown sugar

In a large saucepan, heat oil over medium heat and cook garlic, Italian seasoning, red pepper, salt, and pepper for 1 to 2 minutes. Add tomatoes, and bring to a boil. Reduce heat to low and simmer, uncovered, for 15 minutes, or until the sauce thickens. Remove from heat and stir in nondairy milk and brown sugar. This softens the acidity of the tomatoes. Adjust seasoning to taste.

QUICK BASIL PESTO

MAKES ABOUT ¾ CUP

1 cup packed fresh basil

¼ cup olive oil

1 garlic clove

1 tablespoon lemon juice

¼ teaspoon sea salt

¼ teaspoon freshly ground black pepper

In a food processor, combine all ingredients. Process until smooth.

BASIC BÉCHAMEL

BESCIAMELLA

MAKES ABOUT 3 CUPS

This basic white sauce can be thrown on pasta, pizza, or anything else you think would taste better smothered in cream sauce.

Heat 1 tablespoon of the oil in a medium skillet over medium-high heat. Add onion and let cook until soft. Add garlic and cook for 1 minute. Remove from heat. In a blender, combine onion, garlic, cashews, water, lemon juice, and salt. Process on high until very smooth, about 2 minutes.

1 tablespoon olive oil

1 large onion, chopped

2 garlic cloves, minced

½ cup raw cashews or blanched almonds*

2 cups water

1 tablespoon lemon juice

2 teaspoons sea salt

*If you are not using a high-powered blender, such as a Vitamix, soak cashews or almonds overnight or boil for 10 minutes and drain. This will soften them and ensure a silky smooth cream.

CLASSIC PESTO SAUCE

PESTO ALLA GENOVESE

MAKES ABOUT ⅔ CUP

In a food processor, combine basil, pine nuts, garlic, lemon juice, and salt. Pulse until finely chopped, then drizzle oil and process until smooth. Adjust seasoning to taste.

2 cups packed fresh basil

¼ cup pine nuts, cashews, or walnuts

2 garlic cloves

1 tablespoon lemon juice

¾ teaspoon sea salt

¼ cup olive oil

COSCARELLI MARINARA SAUCE

SALSA ALLA MARINARA

MAKES 4 CUPS

2 tablespoons olive oil

1 onion, finely chopped

1 large carrot, finely chopped

1 cup finely chopped celery

2 garlic cloves, minced

2 teaspoons Italian seasoning

½ teaspoon sea salt

½ teaspoon freshly ground
black pepper

1 (28-ounce) can crushed
tomatoes

¼ cup soy, almond,
or rice milk

1 tablespoon brown sugar
or maple syrup

When I have the time to make marinara from scratch, this is the family recipe I always turn to. It's made with an Italian soffritto (more commonly known in America as a mirepoix), which is a mix of onion, carrot, and celery for excellent flavor.

Heat oil in a large saucepan over medium heat. Add onion, carrot, and celery and sauté until onion is soft and vegetables are lightly browned. Add garlic, Italian seasoning, salt, and pepper, and let cook a few more minutes. Add tomatoes and bring to a boil. Reduce heat to low and simmer, uncovered, for 15 minutes, or until the sauce thickens. Remove from heat and stir in nondairy milk and brown sugar. This softens the acidity of the tomatoes. Adjust seasoning to taste.

SHORTCUT MARINARA

SALSA ALLA MARINARA RAPIDA

MAKES ENOUGH FOR 1 POUND PASTA

1 (26-ounce) jar marinara sauce

¼ cup soy, almond, or rice milk

1 tablespoon brown sugar or
maple syrup

Sea salt

Freshly ground black pepper

Feel free to enhance this quick marinara sauce with sautéed onion, mushrooms, and garlic.

In a large saucepan add marinara sauce, nondairy milk, and brown sugar and heat through. The nondairy milk and brown sugar will soften the acidity of the tomatoes. Add salt and pepper to taste.

CROSTINI

CROSTINI

SERVES 10 TO 12

This is a basic recipe for crostini. Top as desired, or serve with dip or spread.

Preheat the oven to 425°F.

Place bread slices on a large baking sheet and drizzle or brush with oil. Bake for 5 to 8 minutes, or until lightly browned on top.

1 thin baguette, cut into ¼-inch slices on the diagonal

Olive oil for drizzling

GLUTEN-FREE PIZZA CRUST

MAKES 1 LARGE PIZZA

Preheat the oven to 350°F. Lightly brush a large baking sheet with oil and sprinkle with cornmeal.

In a large bowl, whisk flour, cornmeal, xanthan gum, salt, baking powder, and Italian seasoning. Add water, olive oil, and maple syrup, and mix with a large spoon until incorporated. Transfer dough onto the baking sheet and gently form the dough into a large oval, about ¼-inch thick, and form a ½-inch thick rim. If needed, wet your fingertips with cold water to gently pat it down. Brush the entire crust with oil.

Bake for 10 minutes. Remove from oven, top with desired toppings, and bake again for 10 minutes.

1½ cups all-purpose gluten-free baking flour (preferably Bob's Red Mill brand)

½ cup yellow cornmeal

1 tablespoon xanthan gum

¾ teaspoon sea salt

1 teaspoon baking powder

1 teaspoon Italian seasoning

½ cup water

¼ cup olive oil, plus extra for brushing

1 tablespoon maple syrup or agave

HOMEMADE PASTA DOUGH
IMPASTO PER PASTA FATTO IN CASA

SERVES 6

NOTE: If you don't have semolina flour, you can use 2 cups all-purpose.

½ cup silken tofu

2 tablespoons olive oil

2 tablespoons water

1 teaspoon sea salt

1 cup semolina flour

1 cup all-purpose flour, plus extra for dusting

In a food processor, combine all ingredients and process until a ball of dough forms. Transfer to a lightly floured work surface and knead for a few minutes. Cover tightly with plastic wrap and refrigerate for at least 30 minutes.

Cut the dough into 4 equal parts, and work with 1 part at a time. Roll the pasta dough out using a pasta machine, dusting with flour often so that it doesn't stick. Continue to roll it until very thin, or on the number 5 pasta setting.

Cut the dough into desired shape using a sharp knife, pizza cutter, or pasta machine cutter. For pappardelle, cut the pasta dough into ¾-inch-wide strips.

HOMEMADE RAVIOLI DOUGH
IMPASTO PER RAVIOLI FATTO IN CASA

SERVES 6

In a food processor, combine all ingredients and process until a ball of dough forms. Transfer to a lightly floured work surface and knead for a few minutes. Cover tightly with plastic wrap and refrigerate for at least 30 minutes.

Cut the dough into 4 equal parts, and work with 1 part at a time. Roll the pasta dough out using a pasta machine, dusting with flour often so that it doesn't stick. Continue to roll it until very thin, or on the number 4 pasta setting.

Cut the dough into desired shape using a sharp knife, pizza cutter, or pasta machine cutter.

½ cup silken tofu

2 tablespoons olive oil

2 tablespoons water

1 teaspoon sea salt

2 cups all-purpose flour, plus extra for dusting

MOZZARELLA SAUCE

MAKES ABOUT 1½ CUPS

NOTE: Leftovers can be refrigerated for up to 4 days or frozen for up to 1 month and thawed before using.

In a blender, combine cashews and water. Blend on high until very smooth, about 2 minutes. Add lemon juice, salt, garlic, onion powder, and cornstarch, and blend until smooth.

1½ cups raw cashews*

1 cup water

2 tablespoons lemon juice

1½ teaspoons sea salt

1 garlic clove

1 teaspoon onion powder

2 tablespoons cornstarch

*If you are not using a high-powered blender, such as a Vitamix, soak overnight or boil for 10 minutes and drain. This will soften them and ensure a silky smooth cream.

HERBED GARLIC TOAST
PANE TOSTATO ALL'AGLIO CON ERBE AROMATICHE

SERVES 4 TO 6

¼ cup olive oil

1 tablespoon nutritional yeast flakes

3 garlic cloves, crushed

½ thin baguette, cut into ¼-inch slices on the diagonal

Sea salt

Italian seasoning for sprinkling

Combine oil, nutritional yeast, and garlic in a small bowl. Stir until combined.

Spread the garlic mixture over each piece of bread. Sprinkle salt and Italian seasoning over each half and broil for 1 to 2 minutes, checking very frequently until desired crispness. Keep your eyes on the toast—it can burn very quickly!

HOMEMADE CHILI OLIVE OIL
OLIO DI OLIVA AL PEPERONCINO

MAKES 1 CUP

1 cup olive oil

1 tablespoon crushed red pepper flakes

Combine oil and red pepper in a medium saucepan and heat over low for about 5 minutes. Remove from heat, let cool, and store in a sealed jar or bottle in the refrigerator. Infused oil will last up to 1 month.

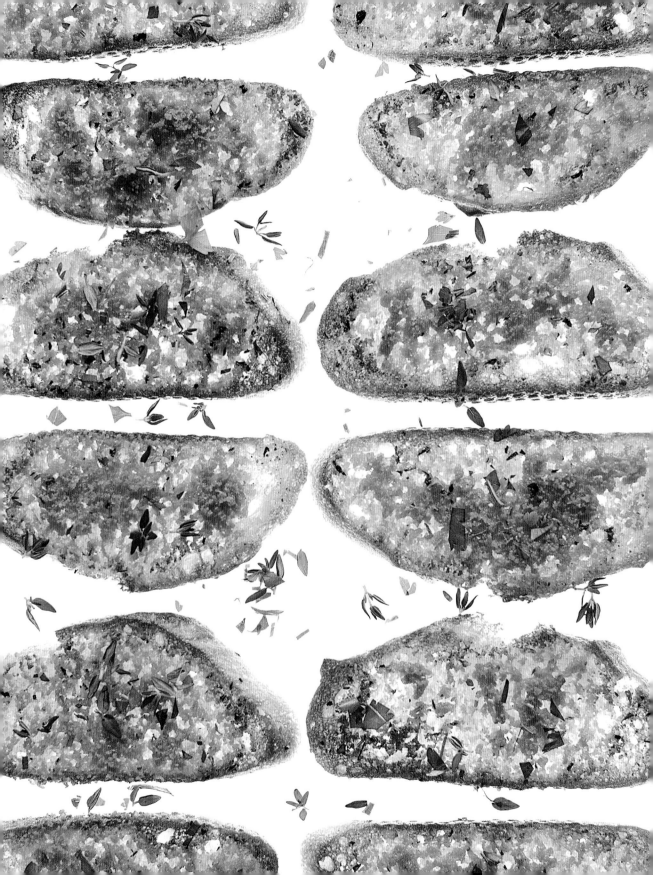

PIZZA DOUGH

MAKES 1 TO 1½ POUNDS

In a small bowl, dissolve yeast in water. Let stand until bubbles form, about 10 minutes.

In a large bowl, combine flour, oil, salt, sugar, and the yeast mixture. Using lightly floured hands or an electric mixer fitted with a dough hook, mix until a stiff dough has formed. If the dough is too sticky, sprinkle extra flour, 1 teaspoon at a time, as needed. Place the dough in a large well-oiled bowl and rotate the ball of dough so it is completely covered with the oil. This will prevent the dough from sticking to the bowl as it rises. Cover with a dry kitchen towel and place in a warm part of the kitchen until it has doubled in volume (1 to 1½ hours).

Place dough on a lightly floured work surface, shape into a disk, and knead for 5 minutes using the steering wheel technique* (see below). Use dough immediately or cover tightly in plastic wrap and refrigerate or freeze for a later use. Thaw to room temperature before using.

*Steering Wheel Technique: Shape dough into a disk and place one hand at twelve o'clock (top of the disk). Fold dough in half toward six o'clock. With the heel of your hand, press the dough from six o'clock to twelve o'clock. Turn dough a quarter of a turn. Repeat process for 5 minutes.

1 package active dry yeast (2¼ teaspoons)

1 cup warm water (about 110°F)

2½ cups all-purpose flour (or half all-purpose flour and half whole wheat flour), plus extra for rolling

1 tablespoon olive oil, plus extra for brushing

1 teaspoon salt

1 tablespoon sugar or maple syrup

SHIITAKE BACON
PANCETTA DI SHIITAKE

MAKES ENOUGH FOR A POUND OF PASTA

Use this as a topping for any pasta or pizza recipes.

1 pound shiitake mushrooms, stems removed and thinly sliced (about ¼ inch thick)

¼ cup olive oil

1¼ teaspoons sea salt

½ teaspoon freshly ground black pepper

Preheat the oven to 375°F.

On a large rimmed baking sheet, toss mushrooms with oil, salt, and pepper. Bake for about 30 minutes, turning frequently with a spatula, until lightly browned and crisp.

ROCKIN' RICOTTA
RICOTTA

MAKES ABOUT 3 CUPS

One of the joys of being Italian American is bringing American ingredients into traditional Italian food. Tofu is a wonderful vegan ingredient that lends a ricotta-like consistency.

MAKE-AHEAD TIP: Ricotta can be made the day before and stored in the refrigerator.

1 tablespoon olive oil

1 large onion, roughly chopped

3 garlic cloves

1 (14-ounce) package extra-firm tofu, drained

2 tablespoons lemon juice

2 teaspoons sea salt

1½ teaspoons freshly ground black pepper

3 cups fresh basil

In a large skillet, heat oil over medium heat and sauté onion until soft. Remove from heat.

In a food processor, combine onion, garlic, tofu, lemon juice, salt, pepper, and basil. Pulse until ingredients are just combined, but mixture still has some texture. Seasoning to taste.

PARMESAN TOPPING

PARMIGIANO

MAKES ABOUT ¾ CUP

Use this as a topping on pastas and pizzas, just as you would with Parmesan cheese. Store in the freezer for up to 6 months and use as desired.

½ cup blanched almonds

1 tablespoon nutritional yeast flakes

½ teaspoon sea salt

1 teaspoon maple syrup

In a food processor, combine almonds, nutritional yeast, and salt, and process until a fine meal forms. Drizzle in maple syrup, and pulse until incorporated.

TOASTED BREAD CRUMBS

PANE GRATTUGIATO TOSTATO

MAKES ½ CUP

Top on pasta or vegetables for a delicious crunch. Bread crumbs can be stored in the freezer.

2 teaspoons olive oil

½ cup Italian bread crumbs

Sea salt

In a large skillet heat olive oil over medium-high heat. Add bread crumbs and season with salt. Toast until lightly browned, stirring often to prevent burning.

COCONUT WHIPPED CREAM
PANNA MONTATA AL COCCO

MAKES ABOUT 1½ CUPS

NOTE: For best results, coconut whipped cream should chill in the refrigerator for a few hours or overnight before serving.

Chill the bowl and whisk of a stand mixer in the freezer for about 10 minutes. If they are not very cold, the cream will not whip properly. Skim the solidified coconut cream from the chilled can of coconut milk and transfer the solids to the bowl of the stand mixer. Do not include any of the coconut water, even if you have to leave behind a little margin of coconut cream (a little bit of coconut water can harm your results).

Add powdered sugar and whip for a few minutes until the mixture begins to stiffen and turn into whipped cream. Chill the whipped cream in a covered container in the refrigerator. It should firm up even more as it sits in the refrigerator for the next few hours or overnight.

1 (13.5-ounce) can of coconut milk (not light), preferably Thai Kitchen brand or Whole Foods 365 brand, chilled in the refrigerator overnight (be sure not to shake or stir)

½ cup powdered sugar

CHOCOLATE GANACHE
CREMA DI CIOCCOLATO

MAKES ABOUT 1 CUP

Melt chocolate chips and nondairy milk in a double boiler or microwave. Whisk in oil until smooth.

1 cup semisweet chocolate chips (dairy-free)

¼ cup coconut, almond, or soy milk

2 tablespoons canola oil

CHLOE'S VEGAN "NUTELLA"

"NUTELLA" VEGANA

MAKES ABOUT 2½ CUPS

MAKE-AHEAD TIP: Can be made in advance and stored in the refrigerator for up to 1 week. Soften at room temperature before using.

Melt the chocolate chips in a double boiler or microwave until smooth. In a food processor, pulse almonds until very fine and powdery. Add melted chocolate, almond extract, and nondairy milk. Process until very smooth. There will still be tiny bits of almonds in the mixture, but try to get it as smooth as possible.

1 cup semisweet chocolate chips (dairy-free)

1 cup almonds, with or without skins

½ teaspoon pure almond extract

¼ cup soy, almond, or rice milk

CHLOE'S TIP:

Nutella is one of those foods that you might think would be vegan, but actually this delicious spread contains chocolate, hazelnuts, and milk. My version uses dairy-free chocolate chips and almonds, which are less expensive than hazelnuts.

VEGAN ITALIAN PANTRY

Here's a breakdown of all the ingredients you need to know to make vegan cooking easy peasy. Lucky for you, the beauty of Italian food is in the simplicity of its ingredients, so you won't need a dictionary to understand this list!

NUTS

Nuts of all kinds are essential to Italian cooking, whether they're almonds, cashews, walnuts, pine nuts, or pistachios. They are not only a key ingredient in pesto sauces and many Italian desserts but also a wonderful cream and cheese substitute in vegan cooking. When blended with water and other flavors, almonds can make a creamy Alfredo sauce, and cashews can make a luscious mozzarella sauce. If you are allergic to nuts, see page 4 for substitutes.

FATS AND OILS

Olive Oil

The most commonly used oil in Italian cooking and baking, olive oil is rich in antioxidants and vitamin E. It is a great source of heart-healthful monounsaturated fat and helps to lower cholesterol. Olive oil is a good choice for medium-heat cooking, such as sautéing and browning. It is also great in salad dressings and sauces, and for drizzling on finished dishes. I prefer extra-virgin olive oil, which comes from the first pressing of olives, making it the purest in taste and least acidic. In my recipe for Homemade Chili Olive Oil (page 238), I infuse olive oil with crushed red pepper. This is my favorite kind of olive oil to drizzle on pizza and pasta to give it a kick of heat.

Canola Oil

Canola oil is my go-to cooking oil for baking or high-heat cooking. It is low in saturated fat yet high in healthful omega-3 fatty acids. It is very mild tasting and has a high smoke point. All of these qualities make it an excellent choice for cooking, baking, or frying at high temperatures. Other mild-tasting oils include vegetable, safflower, and grape-seed oil, which can all be used in place of canola oil.

Coconut Oil

Coconut oil, which is pressed from copra (dried coconut meat), is one of the few saturated fats that does not come from an animal and is actually very healthful. It is high in lauric acid, which has many antiviral, antibacterial, and antioxidant properties that fight ill-nesses such as heart disease, diabetes, cancer, and HIV. It is also cholesterol and trans fat free. Because coconut oil is quite heat stable, it is perfect to use for high-heat cooking or frying. It can keep on your pantry shelf for up to two years.

Coconut oil is solid at room temperature, which makes it great for baking. Unrefined coconut oil has a coconut flavor, while refined coconut oil does not. Feel free to substitute refined coconut oil for vegan margarine or vegetable shortening in equal proportions in my recipes. It works especially well as a substitute in my frostings and cookies.

Vegan Margarine

Vegan margarine is a terrific substitute for butter in vegan cooking and baking. My favorite brand of vegan margarine is Earth Balance, and it can be purchased in sticks or in a tub. It's made from a blend of oils and comes in soy-free varieties. It is all natural, nonhydrogenated, and trans-fat free. You can buy it at your local grocery store or natural foods market.

Nonhydrogenated Vegetable Shortening

Shortening is a solidified blend of oils that is great for making creamy frostings and flaky pie crusts. To make sure you are choosing the most healthful option, look for packaging that says "nonhydrogenated." Spectrum Organics and Earth Balance are excellent brands.

FLAVORINGS

Herbs

Herbs are essential to Italian cooking, and I use both fresh and dried. The conversion is one part dried to three parts fresh if you need to substitute. The most common Italian herbs are basil, parsley, thyme, and rosemary. Remember to buy Italian flat-leaf parsley for the recipes in this book (not curly parsley, which is usually found as a garnish on diner omelets)!

Capers
Capers are the pickled buds of the caper bush. They are pickled in salt or a vinegar brine and are quite pungent. Capers are delicious as an anchovy substitute in Italian cooking because of their tangy, salty flavor. They can be found in jars in the pickle and olive section of most grocery stores.

Nutritional Yeast Flakes
Not to be confused with brewer's yeast or yeast used to make dough rise, nutritional yeast has a roasted, nutty, cheeselike flavor. It is a good source of amino acids and B vitamins, and most brands are naturally gluten-free. Nutritional yeast is what gives my Pesto Mac 'n' Cheese (page 134) its yellow color and cheesy flavor. You can find nutritional yeast in the bulk aisle in most natural foods markets, or in the Whole Body (supplements/wellness) section of Whole Foods Market. Bob's Red Mill, KAL, and Bragg are excellent brands that can also be purchased online.

Salt
Salt brings out and brightens the flavors of food. I like to cook with fine-grained sea salt, which is unrefined, unbleached, and rich in health-supportive trace minerals. The taste is also far superior to white table salt. Fleur de sel is a moist, hand-harvested sea salt from France that is best used as a finishing salt as in my Dark Chocolate Crostini with Sea Salt and Orange Zest (page 185).

Soy Sauce
Soy sauce adds flavor, saltiness, and color to many vegan dishes. Shoyu and tamari are two variations. Shoyu is a natural soy sauce made from fermented soybeans and grains; tamari is wheat-free. Gluten-free tamari can be found at your local natural foods market and used in place of soy sauce. San-J is a popular brand that carries organic gluten-free soy sauce.

Vinegar
Vinegar is an acidic liquid seasoning that adds tanginess and flavor to food. In Italian cooking, a drizzle of balsamic vinegar ("aged" for a sweeter flavor) on top of a finished dish can brighten the dish and make the flavors come alive. Vinegar is also used fre-

quently in vegan baking to replace eggs. When combined with baking soda, vinegar helps baked goods bind and rise. The types of vinegar that I use most often are white, apple cider, balsamic, malt, and rice.

FLOURS

Wheat Flour
There are a variety of flours to cook and bake with. Many of my recipes call for unbleached all-purpose flour. This is also known as regular white flour, and it yields a light and tender product. I use it in baked goods, and pasta and pizza dough. Whole wheat pastry flour is an unrefined alternative to all-purpose flour. If you prefer, you can use half whole wheat pastry flour and half unbleached all-purpose flour.

Semolina Flour
Semolina flour is a coarse grind of durum wheat, commonly used to make fresh pasta and other "from scratch" Italian wheat products. Semolina gives fresh pasta a nice bite, and prevents a gummy texture.

Cornmeal
Cornmeal, or polenta, is a flour made by grinding dried corn kernels. The two most common types of cornmeal are yellow and white, with yellow being a little bit sweeter. Yellow cornmeal is delicious cooked on the stovetop, as in my Creamy Polenta with Roasted Vegetable Ragù (page 158). I also use yellow polenta on the bottom of my baked breads and pizza crusts for an extra crispy crust and to keep the crust from sticking to the pan.

Gluten-Free Flour
Bob's Red Mill Gluten-Free All-Purpose Baking Flour is an excellent product that can be substituted measure-for-measure in many of my recipes. It is made from a blend of garbanzo flour and potato starch, and can be found at your local grocery store or ordered online at BobsRedMill.com. There are many brands of gluten-free flour, but I find that I get the best results with Bob's Red Mill. When substituting gluten-free flour in a recipe, make sure that the other ingredients you are using in the recipe are labeled gluten-free as well, such as chocolate chips, extracts, baking powder, and so on.

Note that while gluten-free flour can be used in almost all of my dessert recipes with excellent results, it is very important to add xanthan gum (page 257) as directed in the recipe. Also, baking time may vary when using gluten-free flour.

GRAINS

A grain is a small, hard seed that comes in many different varieties. The most common grains are wheat, rice, rye, barley, and corn. Quinoa is considered a super grain. It is a complete protein because it contains all eight essential amino acids.

LEGUMES

The legume family includes beans, lentils, peas, and peanuts. They are a good source of protein and fiber. In Italian cooking, white cannellini beans and lentils are particularly popular.

MEAT SUBSTITUTES

Tempeh

Tempeh (pronounced TEM-pay) is a fermented soy product that is extremely high in protein and fiber. It originates from Indonesia and has a nutty texture and mild flavor. Don't be alarmed if you see black spots on the tempeh. That is a completely normal sign of the fermentation process. Opened packages of tempeh will keep for up to ten days in the refrigerator and up to three months in the freezer. Tempeh can be crumbled, sliced, diced, or marinated, and used as a meat substitute. It can be found in the refrigerated section of your local natural foods market next to the tofu.

Seitan

Seitan (pronounced SAY-tan) is made from the protein in wheat flour called gluten. It is chewy, hearty, and soaks up savory sauces very well. It is made from a simple process of mixing wheat flour and water, and you can buy it packaged at your local natural foods market. If you want to make your own seitan from scratch, check out the recipe in my first book, *Chloe's Kitchen*.

Tofu

Commonly used in vegetarian cooking, tofu is high in protein and iron and very low in calories and fat. It is made from soybeans and will take on the flavor of any dressing, marinade, or sauce, making it a versatile meat substitute. There are two kinds of tofu that I like to cook with: soft and extra firm. Soft (or silken) tofu is great for blending into salad dressings or dips. Extra-firm tofu can be crumbled, baked, and stir-fried. Any leftover tofu can be kept in a container, covered in fresh water, for up to five days in the refrigerator. Change the water every two days. Tofu freezes well. When thawed, the texture will be firm and chewy, which makes it perfect for savory dishes.

MUSHROOMS

Mushrooms are the only vegetable that I am addressing in the pantry because they have a juicy and meaty texture, making them a fabulous choice in vegan cooking. They are rich in antioxidants, protein, and fiber. Mushrooms are also a great source of minerals, such as selenium, that fight heart disease and cancer. Choose mushrooms that are firm and dry, and wipe them clean with a damp towel. Trim the stem ends of all mushrooms before using. Remember that the stems of shiitake mushrooms are not edible. The mushrooms I use most frequently are cremini, portobello, baby bella, shiitake, oyster, and porcini.

NONDAIRY MILK

There are many varieties of nondairy milk including soy, almond, rice, and coconut. They are healthful low-fat alternatives for anyone who wants to avoid dairy. Nondairy milks are often enriched with vitamins, and are free of cholesterol and lactose. They come in plain, unsweetened, chocolate, and vanilla. You can purchase nondairy milks in refrigerated cartons or aseptic containers, which do not have to be refrigerated until opened and are perfect for lunch boxes and traveling.

Soy Milk
Soy milk is made from soybeans and water and has almost as much protein as cow's milk but is cholesterol free and low in saturated fat.

Almond Milk
Almond milk is made from pulverized almonds and water. The almond flavor is very subtle. Almond milk is thick and has added vitamins, such as calcium and vitamin D. It has no saturated fat, is cholesterol free, and very low in calories.

Rice Milk
Rice milk is a great alternative for those who are allergic to nuts or soy. Milled rice is mixed with water, creating a thinner milk, and is enriched with vitamins. It is low in sodium, has no saturated fat, and no cholesterol.

Coconut Milk

Coconut milk is thick and creamy, making it a great nondairy milk to use in Asian sauces, curries, and desserts. The fat in coconut milk is a healthful, so-called good fat, does not contribute to heart disease, and is beneficial to the cardiovascular system. You can buy coconut milk canned or in cartons in the refrigerated section of your grocery store. I prefer to use canned coconut milk, which is slightly thicker. With the exception of my Coconut Whipped Cream recipe (page 245), you can substitute light canned coconut milk, which is lower in fat.

PASTA

I always get asked the same question: "Is pasta vegan?" Well, yes and no. Dried pasta is almost always vegan (except for egg noodles). Fresh pasta, on the other hand, is commonly made with egg. Feel free to use my Homemade Pasta Dough recipe (page 236) for any of my pasta recipes or buy dried pasta from the store. You can use regular wheat pasta ("white" pasta), or you can substitute whole wheat or gluten-free alternatives. Brown rice noodles are made from brown rice and water. They have a slightly softer texture than wheat noodles and are gluten free. They take longer to cook than wheat noodles. You can also use quinoa noodles, which are gluten-free and have a beautiful golden color.

SWEETENERS

Sugar

When choosing granulated or powdered sugar to bake with, I look for words like "organic," "fair-trade," and "vegan" on the package because some refined sugars are processed using animal bone char. Wholesome Sweeteners, Florida Crystals, and Whole Foods are all good-quality brands that make specifically vegan unrefined sugars.

Agave

Agave nectar is a natural, unrefined liquid sweetener that is extracted from the leaves of the Mexican agave plant. Agave has a sweeter flavor than sugar, and a lower glycemic index too. I prefer to use light agave because of its mild flavor and clear color, but you can also buy it in darker varieties.

Maple Syrup

Pure maple syrup is a natural, unrefined liquid sweetener that is good for more than just pouring over pancakes. Its distinct maple taste can enhance many savory dishes and baked goods.

THICKENERS

Xanthan Gum

Xanthan gum is a fine powder that is used in baked goods for thickening, stabilizing, and emulsifying. It is a key ingredient in gluten-free baking. Whenever you use Bob's Red Mill Gluten-Free All-Purpose Flour, it is best to add xanthan gum as directed on the back of the flour package. You can buy xanthan gum from most natural food markets or online at BobsRedMill.com.

Guar Gum

Guar gum is a fine powder that is used for thickening, stabilizing, and emulsifying, mostly in cold foods. I use guar gum when making ice cream from scratch because it adds a thick and stretchy quality to the ice cream. You can buy guar gum from most natural food markets or online at BobsRedMill.com.

Cornstarch and Arrowroot

Cornstarch is a fine powder made from corn kernels. Arrowroot is a fine powder prepared from the root stalks of a tropical tuber. Both cornstarch and arrowroot are used as thickeners in sauces, gravies, and custards. Arrowroot is a great corn-free alternative to cornstarch; they can be used interchangeably.

BAKING

Chocolate Chips

I use semisweet chocolate chips in many of my dessert recipes. They can be used whole or melted. Many brands, such as Ghirardelli or Guittard, make semisweet chocolate chips that are dairy free. You can also buy chocolate chips that are labeled "dairy free" or "vegan" at your local natural foods market.

Unsweetened Cocoa Powder

There are two types of unsweetened cocoa powder: Dutch-processed and natural. Dutch-processed cocoa powder goes through a procedure to soften the acidity of the cocoa, giving it a richer and less bitter flavor. I prefer to use Dutch-processed and recommend brands such as Valrhona or Droste. However, whichever kind of cocoa powder you have available will work just fine, as long as it is unsweetened.

Instant Espresso Powder

Espresso powder is a very dark and strong instant coffee. I use it in many of my dessert recipes for flavoring. I use Medaglia d'Oro brand, which can be found in the coffee aisle at any grocery store or purchased online. If you cannot find espresso powder, you can substitute the same amount of finely ground instant coffee. You may also use decaffeinated instant espresso or coffee.

Flavored Extracts

Adding a teaspoon or two of flavored extract is a great way to intensify flavor. When purchasing extracts, look for the word "pure" such as "pure vanilla extract" or "pure almond extract" to avoid artificial flavors and chemicals.

Shredded Coconut

Shredded coconut, also known as "chopped coconut" or "coconut flakes," adds extra flavor and texture to coconut cakes and pies. Feel free to use sweetened or unsweetened coconut. Toasting shredded coconut adds a little extra crunch to your dessert.

EQUIPMENT

Blender

A blender is an important tool for making cream sauces, pureed soups, ice cream bases, and pasta sauces. You can use any type of blender for the recipes in this book. My favorite is a Vitamix, which is a very high-speed, heavy-duty, powerful machine, available in restaurant supply stores, warehouse stores, and online. A lower-speed blender will work just fine; just be sure to stop periodically and scrape down the sides with a spatula while blending.

Food Processor

A food processor is the workhorse of the kitchen. The processor can help you take shortcuts in your recipes by making pasta dough, chopping nuts, grating zucchini, grinding chocolate, and so on. I recommend getting at least an eleven-cup-capacity food processor, although you can always work with a smaller one in batches.

Parchment Paper

Parchment paper is coated with silicone to make it nonstick. It is available in both rolls and sheets. Use it on baking sheets to prevent baked goods from sticking to the pan. Parchment paper is preferred to waxed paper, which is not always oven safe.

Stand or Hand Mixer

Electric stand mixers are useful for kneading dough, mixing batters, and beating frostings. If you do not have the kitchen space for a stand mixer, a handheld electric mixer will work too.

Ice Cream Maker

Ice cream makers come in a range of shapes, sizes, and prices. You do not need to buy an expensive industrial ice cream maker to make my ice cream desserts.

Ice Cream and Cookie Scoops

Ice cream and cookie scoops are great for scooping dough and batter evenly. This will give your baked goods a professional, uniform look. For scooping cookie dough, I prefer a one- or two-tablespoon scoop. For scooping cupcake batter, I prefer a four-tablespoon scoop for regular-size cupcakes and a one-tablespoon scoop for mini cupcakes.

Baking Sheets and Cake Pans

Baking sheets and cake pans come in different shapes and sizes, but I recommend keeping these on hand:

- Two 9-inch round cake pans

- One 9 x 13-inch pan

- One 8-inch square pan

- Two or three large rimmed baking sheets

- Two 12-cup cupcake pans

- Two 24-cup mini cupcake pans

CHLOE'S FAVORITE ITALIAN RESTAURANTS AROUND THE WORLD

John's of 12th Street *(New York City)*

Eataly *(New York City)*

La Masseria Ristorante *(New York City)*

Lombardi's Pizza *(New York City; crust is vegan!)*

Vinnie's Pizzeria *(Brooklyn)*

Scarpetta *(New York City, Beverly Hills, Toronto)*

Il Pastaio *(Beverly Hills)*

Purgatory Pizza *(Los Angeles)*

The Original Pizza Cookery *(Los Angeles)*

Bay Cities Italian Deli & Bakery *(Santa Monica)*

Rosti Tuscan Kitchen *(Santa Monica)*

Portobello Vegan Trattoria *(Portland)*

Ristorante Da Mario *(Florence, Italy)*

Pizza & Co. *(Lecce, Italy)*

Ike's Place *(San Francisco)*

ACKNOWLEDGMENTS

Thank you to my innovative editor at Atria/Simon & Schuster, Leslie Meredith. This is our third book together, and I couldn't be more appreciative of your support over the years. To think it all started in our first meeting when we hit it off and you served me delicious vegan cupcakes! A special thank you to my new friends at Atria/Simon & Schuster: president and publisher Judith Curr, associate publisher Benjamin Lee, publicity director Paul Olsewski, assistant publicity director Lisa Sciambra, art director Dana Sloan, designer Kris Tobiassen, publishing manager Jackie Jou, manager of prepress services Raymond Chokov, indexer Elizabeth Parson, and associate editor Donna Loffredo.

Thank you to my oldest friend, Danielle, and her Italian *amore*, Lele, who together have shown me the best sites, food, and hospitality that Italy has to offer. Thank you for helping with the Italian translations in this book! *Ti voglio bene.*

To all my friends, family, neighbors, and roommates, from California to New York City, for attending my taste-testing dinner parties and never getting sick of Italian food. Thank you, Mommy, Daddy, Andy, and Rocio for always being there for me. Daddy and Grandpa—I think this is a book you can really sink your teeth into!

To all my recipe testers and editors: Some of you came from culinary school, others from college, and each one of you were the sharpest knives in the drawer. Thanks for gathering in my New York apartment every Monday to test and feast on a million recipes at a time: vegan mac 'n' cheese expert Tiffani Brown, Tae Richmond-Moll, Sarah Scheffel, Katie Lee, Bridget Doherty, Alyssa Loscalzo, Callie McBride, Nancy Sobel Butcher, Stephanie Kivich, Justine Ma, and Matt and Matthew Monteiro.

Extra-special thanks to:

Ann Marie Monteiro: You handpicked and managed an unstoppable recipe-testing team from around the nation, and I am forever grateful. It is because of your hard work that I am confident every recipe in this book is perfect.

Susan Antoniewicz: You were willing to go where no tester has ever gone before. You were a whiz at using our test kitchen pasta attachments and made homemade pastas like it was nobody's business. You took on the most challenging tasks and performed them with ease.

Hugs and much appreciation to: my wonderful literary agent, Janis Donnaud; fabulous cover photographer Miki Duisterhof; sweet food stylist Mariana Velasquez; Steven Boljonis; creative food photographer Teri Lyn Fisher; detail-oriented food stylist Jenny Park; hip makeup artist Sheri Terry; color-coordinated fashion stylist Ava E. Naimi; my amazing culinary school, the Natural Gourmet Institute; man-at-the-ready Aaron Lea; photographer Roberto Raphael; grammar guru Linda Wolvek; Carisa Hays, Anna Bolek, Josh Saviano, the Sohaili family, Anna and Jesse Nabel, Esha and Nitasha Ranganath, Ritu Ghai, Tiffany Wong, Natasha Hwangpo, Monica Malaviya Bhuva, Deepti Chauhan, Dani Kaiserman, Samantha Johnston, Azadeh Sinai, Danielle Farzam, Naz Farahdel, Laura Alexander, Laura Frischer, Michelle Khedr, Victoria Yeliokumson, Niki Desai, Cindy Flores, Sandhya Jacob, Neera Khattar, Lisa Bloom, Brooke and Mike McMahan, Cesare Gagliardoni, April Connelly, Nancy and Jerry Feldman, and Bountiful Home for my beautiful cake stands.

To you, for not only reading the recipes in this book, but making it as far as the acknowledgments! You are extra special!

Last but not least, to my good friends Tagliatelle, Fettuccine, Cavatelli, and Orecchiette, for always encouraging me to use my noodle, stay saucy, and never be cheesy.

Grazie!

INDEX

Note: Page references in *italics* indicate photographs.

ABOUT THE AUTHOR

Chloe Coscarelli is a graduate of the Natural Gourmet Institute for Health & Culinary Arts, the University of California, Berkeley, as well as Cornell University's Plant-Based Nutrition Program. She is the author of *Chloe's Kitchen* and *Chloe's Vegan Desserts*, and creator of ChefChloe.com. She divides her time between New York City and Los Angeles.